How to Pray

How to Pray

Dr. Ronnie W. Floyd

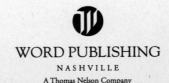

WORD PUBLISHING

NASHVILLE

A Thomas Nelson Company

I want to dedicate this book to every person who has ever
prayed for me. To the thousands who have ever uttered my name
before the Father, I dedicate this book to you.

You can show this book to others and say to them, "Look, this book has
been dedicated to me." Although your individual names are not recorded,
due to my inability to know who has ever uttered my name in the Father's
presence, you can testify to others that you have prayed for me.

May God bless you for lifting me before the Father continually.
Thanks for being a part of the army of prayer warriors for me.

━ ━ ━ ━

Unless otherwise indicated, Scripture quotations are taken from the *New American Standard Bible*
(NASB), © 1960, 1977 by The Lockman Foundation. Used by permission.

Other Scripture references are from the following sources:

The King James Version of the Bible (KJV).

The New King James Version (NKJV), © 1979, 1980, 1982, Thomas Nelson, Inc., Publishers.

Library of Congress Cataloging-in-Publication Data

Floyd, Ronnie W., 1955–
    How to pray / by Ronnie Floyd.
      p. cm.
    ISBN 0-8499-3746-9
    1. Prayer—Christianity. I. Title.
BV210.2.F6 1999
248.3'2—dc21

                                    99–20347
                                    CIP

Printed in the United States of America
99 00 01 02 03 04 05 QPV 9 8 7 6 5 4 3 2 1

CONTENTS

ACKNOWLEDGMENTS

By God's grace I am what I am. By God's grace I am very blessed.

Thank you, Lord Jesus Christ, for your grace in the past, in the present, and in the future. Without you and the Holy Spirit teaching me some things about communicating with the Father this book would not exist. So thank you, Lord.

I want to thank my wonderful and supportive wife, Jeana. She travails with me during the times I write. She prays for me and supports me. She always reminds me that I do not have to do it all in one day. I love you, Jeana. Thanks for what you add to my life.

I want to thank my two young champions, Josh and Nick. You provide me joy beyond words. Whether you are on the football field, or riding in the car together, or on a family trip, or just sitting at the table as a family, both of you are such a blessing to your mother and me. Thanks for praying for me, supporting me, and encouraging me. You are the best—my heroes.

I want to thank my Assistant Gayla Oldham and my Director of Children's Choir Ministries, Anita Stewart. These two ladies have gone through the manuscript of this book before it was sent to the publisher. They have sacrificed time, energy, and time with their families to assist in this project. So, to Gayla, Tony, and Lauren Oldham, and to Anita, Ray, Phillip, Matthew (Tank), Alyssa, and Katie Stewart I want to thank you for your investment in teaching others to pray by being a part of this book.

I want to thank the First Baptist Church of Springdale, Arkansas. Thank you for your support and love for me as we pursue the Father together through the means of prayer.

I want to thank the staff of this great church for carrying the load daily. Especially during those times while I am hiding away for a day of writing and I am not always available. Bless you for your service, love, and support.

Finally, thanks must be given to Word Publishers. I have prayed for this opportunity. Whether you have given assistance and direction in writing, marketing, or selling this book, I want to say thanks. You are God's chosen avenue to present this book to Christians all over the world. I have been faithful in the stewardship of writing it and I am praying for you to be faithful in the stewardship of making it available to the world. By the way, thanks to each one of you that read it. While you read it, pray for me. I am praying for you.

INTRODUCTION

There is nothing like a defining moment in your life. I'm sure you can think of several life-changing moments in your own life. Maybe it was a time of celebration like when a child was born into your family. Or maybe it was a moment of tragedy like when you walked away from a cemetery, knowing that your loved one was buried in the dark, cold earth. A defining moment is a turning point in your life. It's a moment when time appears to stop and God takes you to school. It's a time when your life is shaped, sometimes even transformed.

I clearly remember a defining moment in my life that occurred during the closing weeks of my freshman year of college. I was so young. I was open and willing to do the will of God. I came to college not knowing one soul. Quite honestly, I did not have a clue about what I was getting myself into. I was on fire for God. My passion was alive, and His calling was so clear to me.

During my first year in college, I met fellow students who were in love with God just like I was. We wanted to please God. We wanted to grow. Many times our personal passion for God exceeded our commitment to academics. This passion to please God compelled me to accompany a friend to the Dallas/Fort Worth metroplex to attend a Bible conference in which his father was one of the speakers. Little did I know, but God had designed this experience to shape my entire life and ministry.

This defining moment did not occur inside of a worship center as a response to a biblical message. It occurred late one evening in a restaurant at which my friend's father had arranged for us to spend some private time with a godly man. My physical hunger was great, but my spiritual hunger was even greater. As I listened to this man share his wisdom with us, I was even more encouraged to go on with God.

My friend's father had instructed us to ask this godly man anything we wanted. I was eager to learn how to be a godly minister, so I asked him a question somewhat like this, "Sir, if there is one thing we need to know as young preachers, what is it?" His penetrating eyes looked into mine, and he said, "Ronnie, if you will learn to spend one hour a day with God, there is no telling what God may choose to do with you."

I did not have any better sense than to take that man at his word. Since that day in 1975, I have honored his challenge to me almost daily. His challenge for me to pray on a daily basis stirred me. Even though I did not know then what I know today about prayer, I wanted to be a man of prayer.

That night, God began to define who I was to be as a man of God. What appeared to be just a late-night meal in a restaurant became a turning point for me. It was a "God moment." Truly, it was one of the most defining moments of my life.

My lifelong journey toward serious prayer began that evening. I had already taken an introductory prayer course in my college studies. However, on this particular spring evening in Texas, I began "Prayer 101," a simple introduction to a never-ending call to prayer.

Since that time, I have witnessed God's involvement in my life in many ways. I have seen God heal my wife from cancer. I have seen God move in the lives of both of my children by using them as instruments to win others to Christ. I have seen God interrupt church services with His power. I have seen God bring true revival to His people.

I have also experienced the discipline of God upon my life for my pride. I have experienced what it is like to walk with God through extended periods of fasting and prayer. I have known what it is like to be amazed at how God chooses to use me. I have felt His power upon me in preaching to a few dear folks in my first church in Cherokee, Texas, and have experienced His power to use me in preaching to more than one million men in Washington, D.C. By His grace, I have experienced God's involvement in my life and ministry.

Why has this occurred? I am not someone enabled with great gifts. I do not have the charisma that marks many great leaders. I am confident that it goes back to the defining moment that took place in that restaurant in 1975. I have seen God move in my life because I have been obedient to God's call to prayer.

I have not always known, and still do not know today, all the ins and outs of prayer. I am not a prayer guru. I am just like you. I, too, am on a journey of learning what it is like to commune with God through prayer. I come to God each morning with the same request His disciples made of Him: "Lord, teach [me] to pray" (Luke 11:1).

My purpose for this book is to give you a vision and a hope for prayer. Through my own study and journey of prayer, God has allowed me an opportunity to inspire, assist, and equip you in the ministry of prayer. You can pray. You can pray consistently and effectively. In fact, in the last chapter of this book, I will even give you a practical plan on how to pray.

It is my desire to whet your appetite for prayer through my personal experience and the experiences of others. I want to alert you to the reasons so many Christians do not pray so that you will not fall prey to your enemy Satan. I also want to give you some practical ways that you can have a meaningful time with God every day.

I am not interested in presenting a theory about prayer. Prayer is like physical exercise: You need to do it. Most of the time you do not want to do it. But when you do it, you are so glad you did. Just as exercise reminds you to be careful of the things you eat daily, prayer reminds you to be careful of the choices you make daily. Both exercise and prayer are hard work. Both are necessary. However, the need for and benefits of prayer far exceed that of physical exercise.

I want you to experience what it is like to pray according to God's will, rather than treat God like a puppet who responds to your need. I want you to enter the gateway of God's presence through the powerful name of Jesus, rather than tread timidly into the arena of prayer. I want you to understand what it means to recognize the Holy Spirit as a prayer partner and friend, rather than imagine Him as some foe.

Are you ready to go to a new level in your prayer life? You may have a desire to pray, but you may be overwhelmed at how much there is to learn. There is more than I could tell you in a volume of this size. Yet if we are going to journey to a new level of prayer, we must learn what it means to call upon the Lord. What it means to pray things through. What it means to pray for one another. What it means to do warfare praying. What it means to have your prayers empowered by God.

This is a "how-to" book, not a "you-should" book. We are aware that we need to pray. We have known it for years. We need to be instructed on how to pray consistently and effectively. Stay with me, and by God's grace you will develop these prayer skills.

There is not one Christian who at some time has not felt that his or her prayers didn't reach beyond the ceiling. I want to assure you that many of our prayers *are* ineffective. You see, some things are barriers to effective prayer: things like strained relationships, improper motives, or an unrepentant heart. These walls must come down before our prayers go up. The good news is that God wants to use this book to shatter the walls that have kept you from being an effective prayer warrior.

When the walls come down and the prayers go up, God steps in and makes you a person of influence. This influence does not come because of your ability, but it comes because of prayer. That's right . . . you can become a person whom God uses in prayer. It is possible, and I believe it will happen.

A few years ago while sitting at a ball game, I heard the cheer-leaders chant, "Action! Action! We want action! Ac . . . tion." Action is what this book is all about. I am going to assist you in developing your plan of action. That's right! No longer will guilt surround you when prayer is discussed. I will give you a personal prayer plan that will help you become the person of prayer that you have always desired to become. But this plan can only accomplish its intended purpose if you know how to use it and you choose to use it. This book provides a plan. If you do not follow a plan to pray, you will not pray.

May I give you a warning? The last thing that your enemy Satan wants you to do is to learn to pray. He will do whatever it takes to keep you from reading this book in its entirety. He will distract you when you are trying to read this book. The telephone or the doorbell will probably ring. The children will cry. Gardening or television may seem to be more important. He may even choose to make you sleepy while you attempt to read it.

Please understand this: Satan knows that he is in trouble if you learn to pray. He knows that prayer initiates the power of God. He is aware that prayer can wake up the church of God. He hates prayer! He points his artillery straight toward you when he knows you are serious about prayer.

However, do not fret. God is more powerful than Satan. God pursues a relationship with you. He longs for you to abide in His presence.

He eagerly waits for you to talk to Him. When you finally come into His presence, He puts you into a position where you can hear Him when He chooses to say something to you. Prayer positions you to have a listening ear to what God is saying. Are you ready to hear what God is saying to you? If so, continue on and learn . . .

—Ronnie W. Floyd
Springdale, Arkansas

Section
One

An Introduction
to Prayer

Chapter 1

WHAT PRAYER IS ALL ABOUT

The history of God's people is decorated with men and women of prayer. Volumes have been written about men and women of God who knew how to fall before God at the altar of prayer until their prayers were answered. Countless stories have been told about how some of these prayer veterans even gave their lives calling out to the Lord. I know of no greater accolade for any believer on this side of heaven than to be known as a prayer warrior.

As I read about prayer warriors in the Scriptures, I would love to have the boldness of Moses, who represented God's people before the Lord. I am intrigued by the faith of Elijah, who called down the fire of God to consume the false prophets of Baal. I long for the passion of Ezra as he held forth the Word of God and the people fell on their faces before God in repentance, prayer, and fasting. I crave to have the transparency before the Lord that David had in prayer. I know I need to continually practice the brokenness of Nehemiah before God. As well, I have a passion to possess the unwavering nature of Daniel before the Lord in prayer.

When Zacharias prayed about his barren wife Elizabeth, God gave them a son who became the forerunner of Jesus—John the Baptist. What trust Zacharias and Elizabeth exhibited in their prayer life! The disciple Peter had a firm grip on prayer after he was filled with the Holy Spirit at Pentecost. The epistles of Paul to the churches are testimonies of a man who was obviously a true warrior in prayer. Oh, how I desire Paul's insights so I might pray for the church of our day like he prayed for the church of his day!

My life has been further challenged by great prayer warriors who lived after the New Testament days. How I would love to have the courage of John Huss, who was burned at the stake praying to his Master and Lord, Jesus Christ. I am humbled by the faith of George Mueller, who was responsible for feeding the children of his orphanage but never asked for one dime from any man. He just prayed in God's supply. I would love to be consumed with such a burden for America that I could pray like John Knox for his nation: "Lord, give me Scotland or I die!"

The greatest prayer veteran, who modeled what prayer is all about, is Someone we know by name—His name is Jesus Christ.

Each one of these prayer warriors knew what prayer was all about. They were proven veterans of prayer. Time and space will not allow me to mention the countless thousands of other prayer warriors who deserve recognition in a book about prayer.

Yet, as I thought seriously about who could teach us what prayer is all about, I came to one solid, firm conclusion: The greatest prayer veteran, who modeled what prayer is all about, is Someone we know by name—many of us know Him intimately. We have read of His genuine life of prayer, as recorded in the Scriptures. His name is Jesus Christ.

Jesus was a man of prayer. Think about that for a moment. He was the Son of God. He could do anything He wanted to do with His life, but He chose to dedicate His life on this earth to prayer and to service. He personified His deep commitment to prayer before His followers and His enemies. Jesus wanted fellowship with His Father in heaven, and He knew prayer was the only way to experience it.

Jesus provided the following insight into His prayer life: "Truly, truly, I say to you, the Son can do nothing of Himself, unless it is something He sees the Father doing; for whatever the Father does, these things the Son also does in like manner" (John 5:19).

In this scripture, Jesus declared His powerlessness. This is stunning since He was the Son of God. However, Jesus would only be in this powerless state if He were not able to see what the Father was doing. Since we know that Jesus was never powerless, He must have always seen what the Father was doing. He did only that which He saw the Father do in heaven.

How did this kind of fellowship exist between Jesus and His Father in heaven? One word: prayer!

Prayer is the means by which we can know God and His will for our lives. Prayer is our means of communication with God. Prayer is also the way we have spiritual power. All of this is modeled through Jesus Christ.

We can learn so much about prayer from the life of Jesus. Jesus communicated with the Father. But that is not the only element of prayer. The Father also communicated with Jesus. Notice it again: Jesus spoke to the Father. The Father spoke to Jesus. These two realities are what prayer is all about.

A Practical Definition

I want to give you a practical definition of prayer that embodies these two truths about prayer modeled through Jesus' life. The definition is,

Effective prayer occurs when you talk to God and listen to what God is saying to you.

Prayer involves listening to God as much as it involves talking to God. Prayer is a relationship, a fellowship that occurs between you and God. Prayer is the vehicle that takes you into the privilege of experiencing fellowship with God.

Jeana and I have been married for more than twenty years. Through our marriage journey, we have both learned a great deal about what it means to have a relationship with each other. We have learned that our fellowship is not driven by our *commitment* to one another; our fellowship is driven by our *communication* with one another. This communication is marked by each of us talking to and listening to the other. Each of these skills—talking and listening—is valuable and essential in our fellowship as husband and wife.

Even though this is true about marriage, it is even more true in your relationship with God. Do you want to communicate with God? Do you want to be a prayer warrior who is known for praying effectively? If you do, then practice what Jesus modeled in prayer.

Notice the two components of the practical definition of effective prayer that I just gave to you: *talking* to God and *listening* to what God is saying to you. This is what prayer is all about. I want to share with you the talking principles and the listening principles of prayer.

The Talking Principles

Many of you will be familiar with the talking principles of prayer. A real student of prayer is willing to be teachable because he or she is aware that God can always give fresh insights. Take time to think through these talking principles. Do not let your possible familiarity with them move you to skip this section.

Talking to God and *listening* to what God is saying to you. This is what prayer is all about.

Since prayer involves talking to God in a genuine and transparent way, let us investigate the five talking principles of prayer. Although you may have learned these principles in a different order, in this section I will discuss how I incorporate them into my own prayer life. In my prayer time, I usually begin with the talking principle of . . .

Confession

The topic of confession is getting a lot of media attention today. At the writing of this manuscript, our country is going through a major dilemma concerning our president. Not long ago, the president confessed to the American people that he had sexual relations with a young White House intern. As a result, talk shows on television and radio have been bombarded with calls concerning the subject of confession.

In my prayer time, I like to begin with a time of confession. This confession travels along two avenues. The first area of confession that I like to make in my daily prayers is the confession that I am nothing without the Lord. I cry out to God, confessing to Him my helpless state before Him. I declare that I am inadequate and need this time of fellowship with Him in prayer. I often quote the words our Lord spoke to His disciples: "Apart from Me you can do nothing" (John 15:5). I confess daily to the Lord that without Him I am nothing.

The other area of confession that I practice in my daily prayers is the confession of sin. This subject is getting a great deal of discussion among Christ's disciples. There seems to be some confusion about this subject, due to recent teachings about confession of sin.

It is quite obvious to me that Jesus instructed us to say to the Father in prayer, "Forgive us our sins" (Luke 11:4). This statement indicates that Christ's followers are to confess their sins to God. Many Christians are also familiar with the promise of 1 John 1:9: "If we confess our sins, He is faithful and righteous to forgive us our sins and to cleanse us from all unrighteousness." These words of encouragement notify believers of their need for personal forgiveness of sins.

The word *confess* used in the Scriptures is the Greek word *homologeo,* which means "to say the same as God says." Therefore, when we confess our sins, we are saying the same as God says about our sins. As Bible teacher John MacArthur wrote: "To 'confess' our sins in the truest sense involves despising the sin, being grieved by it, and judging it. That is what it means to say the same as God concerning our sin."[1] Confession is more than just admitting to God that you have sinned; it is seeing your sin in view of God's holiness and being as offended by and grieved by your sin as God is. Confession does not involve hiding the truth or shading the truth. True confession is coming clean before God and others about what you have done that is sinful.

For years, when I have confessed my sins, I have attempted to gain God's attitude about my sins. I am grieved that I have violated the privileges given to me by a loving and holy God. I pray, "Lord, my sin deserves death, hell, and the grave. Thank You for judging my sin at the cross. Thank You for forgiving me of my sins." I take the time to ask the Spirit of God to reveal sins that I have committed before others and God. At that point, I ask God to give me His attitude about these sins. I know that God is more concerned about my attitude toward my sin than He is the sin itself.

I have a deep respect and awe for God. Since I am aware of His holy nature, I pray more effectively once I confess my sinfulness before Him and receive His forgiveness. I thank God for the cross, which positions me before Him as a forgiven man.

Once I have worked through the talking principle of confession, I move my prayer time into the principle of . . .

Praise

Once I have spent time before God, confessing to Him my great need for Him and confessing to Him about my sins, my heart is bursting with joy because I am granted His compassion. I am now ready to move into a period of time when I offer praise to God. Praise is expressing your love and adoration for who God is. The attention in praise is not on the hands of God for what He has done for you but on the face of God for who He is.

I love to be around people who accept me for who I am as a person. This is so refreshing in comparison to the vast majority who may want to associate with me because of my title or position.

Since we are made in the image of God, I believe that God wants to be praised for who He is, not just for what He has done for us. I find it very helpful to focus each day on three attributes of God's character, such as His holiness, His mercy, and His love. I take the time to offer praise to God for each one of these attributes. I believe it is also helpful to quote various scriptures to God that emphasize His character or His attributes.

Once I have offered my love and adoration to God for who He is, I turn my attention to the talking principle of . . .

Thanksgiving

Thanksgiving is different from praise. Do not confuse these two talking principles of prayer. Thanksgiving is expressing to God our gratefulness for all of the things He has done for us. Thanksgiving is offering God thanks for the way He has moved in your life and for how He has provided your every need.

When I do something for someone, I like to hear the words, "Thank you." I do not do something for someone for the purpose of being thanked, but I do something for them because I love them.

God loves you. He moves in your life regularly. He does many things for you that you do know and some things that you do not know. He is always active in the life of a believer.

Take time to offer thanks to God daily. Thank Him for a physical blessing He has given to you. Thank Him for a provisional blessing He has given to you. Thank Him for a person He has brought into your life who has blessed you. Thank Him for the spiritual blessings that He freely bestows upon you as you walk with Him and trust Him with the affairs of your life. Discipline yourself to have a thankful heart before God.

The next talking principle of prayer is . . .

Petition

Once my heart is overflowing with thankfulness, I am ready to offer my life to the Lord. I do not think of my personal petitions in prayer as being selfish. When I pray, I am showing my dependence upon the Lord. I believe that God is very interested in me. He wants me to petition Him about whatever is on my heart.

I begin this time of petition by surrendering my entire life to God. I offer Him my mind, my will, my emotions, my spirit, my body, my attitude, my tongue, my motives, my dreams, my goals, my past, my present, my future, my family, and my career. I ask Him to control me with the Holy Spirit. I want to be a Spirit-intoxicated man who is consumed by the leadership and control of the Holy Spirit.

I petition the Lord to make me an anointed man of God. I do not want to be known as "Dr. Floyd," but I want to be known as a man who has a mighty and special touch of God upon his life. I ask the Lord to anoint me with the authority of Jesus Christ so that I might see what He sees, hear what He hears, feel what He feels, and say what He wants said in all situations of life.

At this time of petition, I offer to God several personal requests that may be on my heart about my life, my needs, and my ministry. These might be various problems that I turn over to God and know

God wants to meet. God already knows everything about me. I have tried to discipline myself to have a transparent and open heart before God in prayer. I believe God is attracted to my transparency before Him.

> I petition the Lord to make me an anointed man of God. I do not want to be known as "Dr. Floyd," but I want to be known as a man who has a mighty and special touch of God upon his life.

Through the processes of confession, praise, thanksgiving, and petition, I am prepared to enter a very serious time of prayer that is built upon the talking principle of . . .

Intercession

When I think of intercession, I imagine myself standing in the gap between the God of heaven and the person I am praying for at the time. I want my prayer to be used as the liaison between the two. I believe if God puts a person and his or her need upon my heart, He wants to move in that person's life.

I begin my time of intercession praying for my family. I present each of them and their particular needs before God. For example, my oldest son, Josh, is a senior in high school. I pray about his future every day. My younger son, Nick, will enter high school next year. This critical time of decision in his life is upon my heart as I pray for him.

One of the things I pray for my family each day is for the armor of God to be upon each one of us. I place the teaching of Ephesians 6:10–18 upon each one of us in prayer. This is critical! In the times in which we live, we need God's spiritual armor upon our lives. (I will discuss this in more detail in chapter 10.)

Once I have interceded for my family, I move on to interceding for the needs of my church. As a pastor, I feel God has given me three priorities for my ministry: leading God's people, feeding God's people, and interceding for God's people. I present the needs of God's people before Him in prayer.

In this time of intercession, I have developed a real burden to pray for people who do not know Jesus Christ in a personal way. I pray for people I know by name who do not know Christ. I pray for God to engineer circumstances in their lives through which they will see their need for Him. I pray for God to give me opportunities to build my relationship with them so I might be able to share with them the good news of Christ. I also spend time praying for people I do not know personally who do not know the Lord. God has a heart for people who are lost. I believe I need to pray for their eternal salvation.

I usually conclude this time of intercession by praying for people who have asked me to pray for them or for people whom God puts on my heart on a particular day.

Effective prayer occurs when you talk to God. The five talking principles of prayer are confession, praise, thanksgiving, petition, and intercession. Practice them. Grow in them. Learn from others about them. However, do not forget that effective prayer also involves listening to God.

The Listening Principles

As I said earlier, effective prayer occurs when you talk to God and listen to what God is saying to you. Prayer is not a one-way means of communication that only allows you to talk to God. Prayer is a two-way means of communication in which you talk to God and listen to what He is saying to you.

I want to relate the three listening principles of prayer. I hope you will consider them and begin to practice them in your prayer life if you are not presently doing so. The first listening principle of prayer is to . . .

Be Still and Quiet before God

Since I believe that the Bible is God's primary way of speaking to me, I always attempt to have a Bible near me when I pray. If I want to hear Him, then I must read, know, study, and understand His Word. An open Bible should always accompany a bended knee.

In our rapid-paced and noisy society, it is difficult to be still and quiet before the Lord. Our minds are usually racing a thousand directions, so focus is usually a challenge. Discipline is the only way we can learn to be still and quiet before the Lord.

One thing I really attempt to do is to meditate upon the Scriptures, to think deeply upon His Word. Each day I ask myself this question: "What is God saying to me?" I need to know what God is saying to me through His Word and through the circumstances in my life. I know that God is very committed to His relationship with me. He wants me to know what He thinks. He wants me to know His will. My challenge is to be still and quiet before Him long enough to hear Him speak to me.

At times, it might be healthy for me to have a change of scenery when I am trying to listen to God. Sometimes I just get into my car and drive, without any particular destination, for the purpose of discerning what God may be saying to me. Do whatever it takes to be quiet and still before the Lord. He will say something to you about your life.

This first listening principle of prayer is to be still and quiet before God. The second listening principle of prayer is to . . .

Not Be in a Hurry in Your Time with God

You can grab a hamburger on the run. You can even drive through and get a dessert after you eat your hamburger. On the way home, you can pick up your developed film at the drive-up window of the one-hour photo development store. You can rush here and rush there and become a victim of the hurry disease.

But there is something you must never forget: You cannot be in a hurry in your time with God. You cannot grab a Bible verse like you grab a doughnut on your way to work or school. God does not work like that. He works in His own time.

God wants us to learn to wait before Him. He wants to still our spirits. He wants to silence our hearts. He wants us to learn not to be in a hurry with Him. You will not experience meaningful times with God if you are trying to rush God into your schedule.

On numerous occasions I have had the opportunity to lead worship in various settings, including my own church. Sometimes I feel the schedules have not permitted us to encounter God in such a way that true spiritual freedom exists. Whenever I have the responsibility to lead God's people into spiritual renewal within the context of a rigid, compact, or limited schedule, I always come away unsatisfied with the results. You just cannot rush God.

Learn not to be in a hurry in your time with God. God does not speak on your timetable. He has His own timetable. In His time, He will make Himself known to you. Therefore, learn the power of waiting before Him.

Another listening principle of prayer is to . . .

Spend Various Seasons of Your Life with God

I have discovered the power of setting aside a period of time to be alone with God. In these personal retreats away from the distraction of family, business, and life, I have grown by quantum leaps. God is attracted to someone who will set aside everything else just to be with Him.

A season can be defined in several ways. It can be a period of days in which you devote a select number of hours a day to wait before the Lord. It can be an entire day that you draw aside to be with God. A season can be a time of retreat during which you exit the affairs of this life to be with God for a while. It can be an extended time when you are away from your job or ministry for the purpose of being with God and listening to Him.

I have been on some two- and three-day retreats with God that have profoundly impacted my life. At times, when a preaching assignment is very significant compared to the norm, I will spend time away in a nearby hotel just to be with God and hear Him speak to me.

Remember: Effective prayer involves listening
to what God is saying to you.

Remember: Effective prayer involves listening to what God is saying to you. Consider these listening principles. I promise, they do have the power to change your life. Let God do something new in your life. This fresh work will occur when you learn to listen to what God is saying.

Perspective and Balance

Let me restate the definition of prayer: Effective prayer occurs when you talk to God and listen to what God is saying to you. As I have analyzed, illustrated, and applied this definition in a practical way in this chapter, I hope you will consider the truth of it. Let me tell you quickly the value that it brings in your life of prayer.

When you listen to God as well as talk to Him, you gain a whole new perspective on God. You also gain a new perspective on yourself. By God's grace, you gain a new perspective on the circumstances of your life. If all you ever do is rattle your mouth in prayer, you will never operate with God's perspective in your life.

When you listen to God as well as talk to God, you also are able to maintain balance in your life. Which is more important: what you say to God or what God says to you? The answer is obvious: It is much more important what God says to you. What you say to God will be greatly affected by what God says to you in your life. This is what prayer is all about.

An old adage says, "God gave you two ears and one mouth. Therefore, you should listen twice as much as you talk." That is good advice for life. It is even better advice for prayer.

Chapter 2

WHY CHRISTIANS
DO NOT PRAY

One of the most gut-wrenching races in the sport of track is the four-hundred-meter race. For those who are unfamiliar with this race, four hundred meters is one time around the track. In today's track world, the four-hundred-meter dash is an all-out sprint. Only great, strong athletes can endure the mental and physical challenge of giving it their all for one full lap around the track.

The imperative to being a winning track star on the four-hundred-meter dash is to run the entire race as strong as you began it. The challenge for the athlete is to be so physically fit that the level of exertion is maintained at an optimum level during the entire race. The athlete not physically prepared to run this race cannot keep pace with the conditioned and prepared athletes. He or she may come out of the blocks on that first hundred meters and be in the lead but within moments will be lagging behind.

One of the greatest challenges in the Christian life is to run the entire race with the same intensity that we began it. The problem is that we are not running the entire race with great stamina because we are not fit spiritually to expend all we have for God. We come out of the blocks and look like gangbusters at first, but soon we are lagging behind. At times we are not even on our way toward finishing the race.

One of the most apparent areas of poor performance in the Christian life is the area of prayer. How many times have you said that you were going to become a better prayer warrior? Even though many people have good intentions, they fail to run the race successfully. Initially, they have a great commitment, but in time their intensity wanes. Many times, especially in the area of prayer, their commitment ceases altogether.

A frightening paradox is occurring. One of the most vital spiritual disciplines you need in order to run the entire race with great intensity is prayer. Conversely, one of the most difficult challenges you have in your Christian life is to pray.

It is like knowing that your car cannot run without fuel but discovering the fuel is difficult to obtain. Therefore, you might not always have fuel. Consequently, the car cannot run. What is even more disturbing is that you will have to pay the price to obtain the fuel when you really need to be somewhere else.

Does any of this sound familiar? At times, you may not pray because prayer is difficult. The result is that you have little, if any, spiritual power. Consequently, you live a defeated spiritual life. Yet when things become really difficult, you desperately find a way to pray because you know you cannot make it on your own.

Before we investigate why Christians do not pray, I want you to know two critical statements about prayer:

1. Prayer occurs when you depend on God.
2. Prayerlessness occurs when you depend on yourself.

Will you take the time to read these two statements again? In fact, why don't you commit them to memory right now? These statements are critical in understanding prayer. Prayer occurs when you depend on God. Prayerlessness occurs when you depend on yourself.

People give thousands of excuses as to why they do not pray. No matter what the excuse, the underlying reason is that they love to depend upon themselves. Prayerlessness is always a result of selfishness.

God is calling you to go to a new level with Him. His Spirit is attempting to inspire you to pray more consistently and effectively. Your greatest need and only hope to make a long-lasting difference for God is to learn to pray. Prayer is not an option; it is essential. If you are going to be serious about your faith, then it is imperative that prayer become a major part of your Christian experience.

> Your greatest need and only hope to make a long-lasting difference for God is to learn to pray. Prayer is not an option; it is essential.

If you are going to learn how to be a consistent prayer warrior, then you must understand your obstacles. Even though your self-dependence is the root cause of your prayerlessness, there is more to investigate in this area.

The Four Reasons Christians Do Not Pray

I believe there are four major reasons why Christians do not pray. In this chapter I do not want simply to identify these reasons for you, but I also want to tell you why they exist. One of the major reasons Christians do not pray is . . .

Pride

It was very early on a Sunday morning when God obliterated my pride. I was in the closing days of a forty-day period of fasting and prayer. I could not sleep on Saturday evening, which is a great peril for a preacher. I sensed that God wanted me to interpret my sleeplessness as a call to prayer. Just after midnight, I arose and went into the living room of our home.

Lying prostrate on the floor, I opened my Bible and prayer journal. I asked the Lord what He wanted to tell me. I knew He was up to something. For more than thirty days, I had retreated to be with Him in fasting and prayer. Surely all my sin had been dealt with by now. Little did I know, I was about to experience the awakening of a lifetime.

The Lord guided me to the Book of Isaiah. Before I knew it, my eyes were fixed upon Isaiah 57:15: "For thus says the high and exalted One who lives forever, whose name is Holy, 'I dwell on a high and holy place, and also with the contrite and lowly of spirit. In order to revive the spirit of the lowly and to revive the heart of the contrite.'"

This verse gave me one of the most crushing blows of my entire Christian life. I was filled with fear and shame. It was as if God said, *Ronnie, I dwell in two places: I dwell in heaven and I dwell with the humble. Ronnie, you are not humble but proud. Your pride is the biggest problem in your life. People are not your problem. The church is not your problem. You are your biggest problem. In fact, the biggest problem in your church is you. Repent from your pride immediately. If you really want revival in your church and in your country, you must first repent from your pride.*

This personal message from God was as clear to me that Sunday morning as the day I am writing it to share with you. God meant business. He knew I had a listening ear before Him. He knew I was willing to do anything. It was time for me to understand the real truth about walking with God. God walks with humble people, not proud people. On that early morning, I was embarrassed before God over my pride.

As God's Spirit convicted me, I pleaded guilty. The finger-pointing ceased—I knew that I was the guilty one. If I really wanted to be a man of prayer and a true man of God, I needed to be a humble man. I had tried to be all God wanted me to be for a number of years, but on this particular morning, God exposed the "real me" to me. I have grown from that experience. I still deal with it today.

Pride is the most deceitful sin of all. It cost Adam and the entire human race everything. Pride is so dangerous because it masks a multitude of sins. When pride is exposed, the other sins in your life become like countless snakes coming out of a den. You are not aware of those sins until they are uncovered.

Pride is one of the major reasons we do not pray. Why does pride keep us from praying? **Pride keeps us from praying because it overestimates the power of self.**

Remember: Prayerlessness occurs because you choose to depend upon yourself. Pride keeps you from praying because it overestimates the power of self.

The disciples Peter, James, and John struggled with pride. On the evening before Jesus was arrested, Jesus asked them to pray with Him. They began to pray but ended up sleeping. Three times Jesus asked them to watch and pray, and all three times the disciples fell asleep. This was the most critical night in Jesus' life. Pride is the only sin so deceiving that it could have caused Peter, James, and John to ignore Jesus' personal request. In the middle of the most difficult night of Jesus' life, the disciples had no intensity because they couldn't pray.

Pride kept Peter, James, and John from praying because they overestimated the power of self. They thought they could make it, but within hours, Peter denied Jesus three times. Three times of neglected prayer led to three denials of Jesus. No prayer, no power. No prayer, no courage. No prayer, no victory.

Would you take an inventory of your life right now? Pride is the "self-life." Pride always leads you to point fingers at others. Pride never takes the blame for anything. Pride leads you to think more of yourself than you do of God. Do you have any pride?

God's Word gives us numerous cautions concerning the sin of pride. The writer of Proverbs declares, "A man's pride will bring him low, but a humble spirit will obtain honor" (29:23). And again, "When pride comes, then comes dishonor, but with the humble is wisdom" (11:2).

The caution lights are going off right now. God is warning that pride will always bring you down. The result will be the dishonoring of yourself and the dishonoring of God. None of us would ever do this intentionally, but pride is very deceitful. Be very careful. Pride can sneak into your heart. Before you know it, you will be down and dishonored.

Pride keeps you from praying because it overestimates the power of self. You cannot make it on your own. Your enemy Satan wants you to believe you can. But the result will be prayerlessness and spiritual defeat.

Force yourself to pray. Make yourself go down on your knees. Do whatever it takes to get before God daily. You will never be stronger and your enemy will never be weaker than when you pray.

Another reason Christians do not pray is . . .

Unbelief

When Jesus walked on this earth, He did many mighty and super-natural works. It was in His nature to move beyond the natural. Everyone who demonstrated one small degree of faith experienced the power of God. The New Testament is filled with eyewitness accounts of the mighty acts of Jesus Christ.

However, when Jesus went to His hometown of Nazareth these miracles were limited. The people were amazed at His teaching in the synagogue and asked, "Where did this man get this wisdom and these miraculous powers?" But the Gospel of Matthew makes an interesting observation about this occasion: "He did not do many miracles there because of their unbelief" (13:58).

Jesus impressed the people in Nazareth with His teachings. The only problem was they chose not to believe in Him or His teachings.

As a result of their unbelief, Jesus chose not to do many mighty acts among them. Everywhere He went, the miracles were plentiful—except for places where a lack of faith was prominent, like Nazareth.

There is an element of Nazareth that each of us faces in prayer. There are moments when we just cannot believe. Even though we know about Jesus' ability, we are just not certain that He is willing to intervene in our situation. Rather than choosing to pray, we choose to trust in ourselves. Our unbelief keeps us from praying.

Unbelief is another major reason we do not pray. Why does our unbelief keep us from praying? **Unbelief underestimates the power of God.**

Whereas pride overestimates the power of self, unbelief underestimates the power of God. The result of each of these sins is prayerlessness.

I have had the opportunity to travel across America to speak to various churches, denominational meetings, and conventions. Many times I have felt that God wanted to do something mighty in our midst. Yet, like the synagogue in Nazareth, there is a bondage of unbelief among the people. They simply cannot do what the Spirit is asking them to do because of their unbelief. Instead of believing in the power of God, they make excuses as to why God cannot do the mighty work.

> Whereas pride overestimates the power of self, unbelief underestimates the power of God. The result of each of these sins is prayerlessness.

The eleventh chapter of the Book of Hebrews composes the Hall of Faith, featuring men and women who exercised great faith. Even though many of their circumstances seemed hopeless, they pursued God via prayer. This chapter makes an insightful statement about prayer and its connection with faith: "Without faith it is impossible to please Him, for he who comes to God must believe that He is, and that He is a rewarder of those who seek Him" (v. 6).

According to this scripture, when we pray we must first believe that God is. What does it mean to believe that God is? It means to believe that God is who He says He is and that He can do whatever He says He can do.

When you do not believe that God is who He says He is and that God can do whatever He says He can do, then you do not have faith in God. Without faith, prayer will not occur. Remember: Unbelief underestimates the power of God. Unbelief is a major obstacle to prayer.

Satan wants you to think that God is too busy to listen to your prayers. Your enemy places into your imagination the false idea that God is limited in His power. I trust that you know better. God is who He says He is and He can do whatever He wants to do. He is God!

What are you facing right now in your life that is bigger than you? What is your biggest problem? Does it have to do with business, family, finances, or friendships? God is bigger than your problem.

Therefore, talk to Him about your life. Talk to Him about your problem. There is nothing that God cannot do. When you exhibit even the smallest degree of faith, God will step into your life and care for you through your circumstances. Just as Jesus moved in the lives of those who had faith in Him while He was on this earth, He will move in your life when you exercise faith in Him. Unbelief moves you away from God and prayer. Faith moves you toward God and prayer.

Any reluctance that you have toward prayer is a sign that you are struggling with unbelief. Identify this unbelief for what it is. Refuse to yield to its magnetic hold on your life. God is who He says He is. God can do whatever He says He can do. Therefore, whatever you are facing—big or small—pray!

The third reason Christians do not pray is . . .

Ignorance

Some years after I came to the First Baptist Church of Springdale, Arkansas, God began to open up opportunities to meet some very influential people. I met politicians like former Arkansas congressman John Paul Hammerschmidt, as well as our former governor and two-term president of the United States, Bill Clinton. I also met religious leaders like Billy Graham, Jerry Falwell, and James Dobson.

I will never forget how I felt prior to meeting these people. I would rehearse in my mind what I would say to them. My stomach would churn with stress. I felt that I was out of my league even to carry on a conversation with any of them. I am confident that each of them noticed it. I am certain that some of the things that I said were inappropriate.

My mistake was that I overestimated the difficulty of talking with these influential people. I did not know they were just like me. I was not aware of their desire and interest in others. You see, I made a terrible mistake. I did not know that I could talk to these influential people just like I talked to common people. I did not have to impress anyone. My problem was that I was ignorant—I just did not know any better.

Ignorance is one of the major reasons we do not pray. How does ignorance keep us from prayer? **Ignorance overestimates the difficulty of talking to God.**

God is not difficult to talk to in prayer. Just as I once overestimated the difficulty of talking to influential people, I used to overestimate the difficulty of talking to God. What I know now is that God is easier to talk to than any person. God wants you to talk to Him. He wants you to come to Him anytime, anywhere, and about anything. He wants to fellowship with you.

Forget trying to impress God with your language. He is not interested in your words. He is interested in your heart. Share your heart with God. Real prayer occurs when you share your heart with God. Ignorance can no longer be a reason why you do not pray.

Ignorance is when you do not know any better. Stupidity is when you know better but choose not to do it. Now that you know God is easy to talk to—share your heart with Him. Let Him hear your deepest concerns, regardless of your ability (or lack of ability) to articulate it to Him. Be honest with Him. Let Him hear from you today. It is not difficult to talk to God. Just talk to Him. Respect Him for who He is, but talk to Him just like you talk to other people.

Pride keeps you from praying because it overestimates the power of self. Forsake all of your pride and talk to God. Unbelief keeps you from praying because it underestimates the power of God. Rebuke unbelief and believe that God can do anything in your life. Ignorance keeps you from praying because it overestimates the difficulty of talking to God. Ignorance is no longer an excuse—just share your heart with God.

Another reason people struggle to pray is . . .

Time

Time is one of the most precious commodities you have in life. In the business world, time is money. Each person in this world has 168 hours a week and 24 hours a day. Time places everyone on equal ground.

If you were to ask one hundred people why they do not pray, the subject of time would likely be mentioned. The typical excuse, "I am too busy," is used by the average American to avoid something that they do not deem as important.

One of the major reasons people do not pray is time. How does time keep you from talking with God? **Time underestimates the value of being with God.**

Remember, each person has the same amount of time. Time only becomes the problem when you underestimate the value of being with God.

When I first met Jeana, I was attracted to her immediately. I wanted to spend each waking hour with her. She was very important to me. I had plenty of other things to do; however, I valued spending time with Jeana. Therefore, I always had time for her.

Time with God is essential for life. Whenever you do not take the time to pray, you have a problem with your values. You just do not deem God as important and worthy of your time. Make time to talk to God. Time with God is critical to a successful Christian life.

> Take time for God today. Do not put Him off. He is the King of Kings and Lord of Lords. He is more prominent than any person you will ever meet in life. No one is like Him.

When my schedule becomes cramped with many demands, I always make sure that the first thing I do every day is spend time with God. However, there have been times in the past when my schedule has seemed to force me to cut short my time with God. This has never been beneficial to my day. Rushing my time with God is never advantageous to my spiritual health.

When you take time for God, He will meet with you. Invest your time wisely with God, and He will make your effort worthwhile. Remember what Hebrews 11:6 says: "He is a rewarder of those who seek Him."

Take time for God today. Do not put Him off. He is the King of Kings and Lord of Lords. He is more prominent than any person you will ever meet in life. No one is like Him.

If you heard you could spend some time with Michael Jordan the basketball star, or Bill Gates the computer guru, or Norman Schwarzkopf the military hero, would you rearrange your schedule to spend some time with these people? I guarantee that you would do whatever it took to spend time with one of these people or someone else whom you determined as important. And I bet that you wouldn't just spend a few short minutes with these people; you would want to sit down and talk to them for a long time. What's the point?

The point is that you will spend time with whomever you value in your life. How much do you value God? How much do you honor Him? Do you honor Him with your time? Do you spend time with Him every now and then, or do you value Him enough to spend time with Him every day? Do you take the time to linger with God, or do you give Him merely a token couple of minutes as you fly out the door to go to work or school?

Prayer is your means of spending time with God. It is the way that you express yourself to Him. Never underestimate the value of spending time with God. All God needs with you is a moment. In that moment, He can transform you. He can fill you with hope. God can do more in a moment than you can do in a lifetime.

What is keeping you from praying? Pride? Unbelief? Ignorance? Time? Now is the time to identify what is standing in the way of your becoming a great prayer warrior for God. None of these obstacles are too big to be conquered. Just as David brought down Goliath in the name of the Lord, you can bring down these giants in the name of the Lord.

God wants to be with you. Do you want to be with God? I believe you do, or else you would not be reading this book. Therefore, I want to lead you in how to experience a meaningful time with God each day. It is possible. You can do it! So . . . read on!

Chapter 3

How to Have a Meaningful Time with God

If you could do anything in your life, what would it be? If your time and resources were unlimited, what would you do? I am not talking about something noble or spiritual, but something fun. If my time and resources were unlimited, let me tell you what I would do.

Each Saturday morning, I would board a private jet and fly to the college football game of the week. I would wear the colors of the team I was supporting that day. I would have a great time, sitting in the private box I had rented for the day, accompanied by several friends or family members who had traveled with me.

You see, I love college football. I like the atmosphere. The excitement. The enthusiasm. The glamour. I like it from the beginning warmups to the very end when the last player walks off the field. I love the thrill of victory and dread the agony of defeat.

Football is a special sport because of the many things it can teach its players about life: The value of teamwork. The value of personal performance. The value of having a great work ethic. The value of winning. The value of rebounding from defeat.

One of the constant challenges of a football coach is to keep the team focused on the importance of the fundamentals of blocking correctly, tackling effectively, and running tirelessly. If the offense is pass-oriented, they must allot time each day to throwing and catching the ball. Timing is critical, and the only way to develop this timing is to practice the fundamental of throwing and catching the football daily.

One of the things that makes college football so great is that, on any given Saturday, the "Davids" of the game can defeat the "Goliaths." No one likes to be on the losing end of a major college football upset, but those periodic upsets remind all of us that on any given Saturday anyone can lose.

When the defeated team's college football coach has to face the press in his postgame press conference, he looks as if he has lost his best friend. His team's loss surprises even him. After reviewing the game film, the next day he stands before the alumni and fans in his Sunday afternoon press conference and says something like the following: "Yesterday, we were very disappointed in our team's performance. After reviewing the film, it is obvious that we have got to do a better job of blocking, tackling, running the football, as well as passing and catching it. This week, we are going back to the fundamentals. We will be ready to play next week."

I have heard that speech several times from several of the game's greatest coaches. The "back to the basics" speech is always the key to a dominant team remaining dominant and not losing to the so-called lesser teams on their schedule. One of the key ways to avoid defeat in the game of football is always to do the basics of the game better than your opposition. If you do, victory is likely. If you fail in the fundamentals, defeat is inevitable.

We Are Making It Too Hard

I am convinced that we are making the Christian life a lot harder than God ever intended for it to be. Our enemy Satan has confused our intention, our direction, and our goal. We know that we ought to be winning in the Christian life, yet we are losing much of the time because we are making it too hard.

I believe that the most important action you can take in the Christian life is to have a meaningful time with God daily. This action has got to be the heart of all that we do. It is the most basic of the basics. It is one fundamental that even the greatest Christian had better not fumble, or else defeat is inevitable.

Our enemy's strategy is very deliberate and deceiving. Satan wants to destroy us. He wants to get us out of God's game plan. He wants us to think that living the Christian life is virtually impossible. He has gotten us involved in knowing more about Christianity instead of doing what we know. He has the church of Jesus Christ in disarray over pointless issues that have no positive outcome for the advancement of God's kingdom throughout the world.

It is time to stop "dumbing down" to the devil's level by saying that the Christian life is too hard. This wise and crafty schemer's strategy is very focused. He wants to get followers of Christ involved in so many things that they will not make the time to have a meaningful time with God daily. Some of these things might even be good, but they are not essential.

> We have got to understand that the only way to experience spiritual power, direction, and purpose is to have a meaningful time with God daily.

The issue is not that the Christian life is too hard. The issue is that we are making it too hard. We have got to understand that the only way to experience spiritual power, direction, and purpose is to have a meaningful time with God daily. The only way we are going to defeat the schemes of Satan is to have a meaningful time with God daily. The only way our families and our churches will function properly is for us to have a meaningful time with God daily.

As Christians, we ought to be winning in life. Our enemy has already been defeated through the death and resurrection of Jesus Christ. We already have the victory. We are to be even greater than a dominant football team over its inferior opposition. Like a dominant football team that makes itself vulnerable to defeat by not performing the basics of the game well, we ensure our defeat by neglecting the fundamental of having a meaningful time with God daily.

In this chapter, I am not going to assume that you know how to have a meaningful time with God daily. I am not going to assume that you are a praying Christian who has a strategic plan of prayer for your life. It is obvious by the wreckage of broken lives, broken families, and powerless churches that most Christians are not spending daily time with God. Therefore, I want you to think with me about a few . . .

Special Guidelines for a Meaningful Time with God

The number one priority in the life of a true disciple should be having a meaningful time with God daily. If nothing else gets done in your day, this must get done.

Since a meaningful time with God every day is essential for spiritual victory, we need to learn from every great Christian we know about how to do this. When you meet Christians whom you greatly respect, ask them, "What has helped you have a meaningful time with God daily?" By no means am I a great Christian, but I am a veteran in walking with God. I want to share with you some special guidelines that I have followed that have assisted me in having a meaningful time with God each day.

The first guideline I have discovered is to make your time with God . . .

A Special Time

As I mentioned in the introduction, God taught me the importance of having a time with Him years ago. Even before that defining moment, I strove to have a meaningful time with God daily. Quite honestly, I do not even remember the last day of my life when I did not spend time with God.

All the times we have with God may not be as meaningful as we would like for them to be. Each time my wife and I spend time together is not always as meaningful as we would like for it to be. Yet this does not negate our need as a couple to be together, and it does not negate your need to spend time with God. Sometimes I feel as if many Christians decide not to spend time with God because, for various reasons, the time has not been as meaningful as we expected.

The first guideline to having a meaningful time with God daily is to designate a special time that you meet with Him. It is your most important appointment, and you need to make and to keep it daily. Ask yourself right now, "What time am I going to meet with God every single day for the rest of my life?" Since this is the number one priority in the life of a true disciple, I believe that your appointment with God should take place before anything else in your life.

Your time with God should take place before you read the newspaper each day. It should take place before you turn on the television to watch your favorite morning newscast. Since a meaningful time with God is imperative for you to have a vital relationship with God, then the priorities of your day should reflect this truth. The moment you wander around the house or leave for work or school in the morning without having a meaningful time with God, you make yourself vulnerable to attacks from the enemy.

You have to determine to make your time with God a special time. My time with God happens within moments after I throw water on my face to prepare myself physically for this spiritual activity. It does not matter if it is a routine day for me or a travel day or a vacation day,

God is going to get the prime time of my day. The thing I have learned to do first each day is to spend a meaningful time with God.

In the routine days of life, which normally happen for me on Sunday through Thursday, I have a time set aside for God. I meet God for private devotion at 4:00 A.M. (Yes, God is up at that time.) There may be a slight rescheduling periodically due to travel or schedule, but I always meet with God the first thing every day. This is the rule I follow for Fridays and Saturdays, as well as during vacation time or business travel.

Some of you may protest, "I am not a morning person." It may surprise you, but neither am I. Even if you are not a morning person by nature, it is still important for you to make your time with God the first thing every day. When you meet with God, it shows you depend upon Him. When you do not, it shows you depend upon yourself. If you are going to be involved in effective praying—talking to God and listening to what He is saying—then you must set aside a time for this to happen, or else it probably will not happen.

One of the ways you can make your time with God a special time is for you to work on it being special. By following the remaining guidelines, you can make your time with God special. One guideline that will assist you in making this a special time is to develop the guideline of meeting God at . . .

A Special Place

You may not remember the day or the hour that Christ came into your life, but you will likely remember the place that you surrendered your life to Jesus Christ. I remember the exact place where I repented of my sins and placed all of my faith in Jesus Christ and Him alone for my salvation. Places are very important to God. All through the Scripture, we read various accounts of God's activity, and often the place of the activity receives special attention.

If you are going to have a meaningful time with God every day, then set aside a special place to meet with Him. This special place needs to be somewhere you enjoy. It needs to be somewhere private. The fewer interruptions you have, the easier it is for you to have a meaningful time with God.

I meet with God every day in my study at home. This is my special and private place to be with Him. He has been so real to me in this place. He has spoken to me through His Word. He has built me back up when I have been discouraged. He has put me back together when I am broken. Yes, it is a special place—not because of the color of the carpet, the beauty of the desk, or the books on the shelves. The thing that makes it really special is that it is where God and I hang out together.

Where is the special place that you meet with God? It does not have to be in a private study. It can be on a worn-out lounge chair that sits beside a dim light. It can be at the kitchen table. It may be in your bedroom. For some, it could be on the outside porch. Wherever you meet God is a special place. Meeting Him daily at the same place will make that place very special over the course of time. Let this place be your hiding place, a private place you meet with God.

A Special Plan

If you do not have a plan to meet with God and pray, then you probably will not do either one. If you are going to have a meaningful time with God daily, you need to develop a game plan.

Every day is game day for the Christian. There are no off-days or off-seasons. In order to be ready for your game day every day, you need to follow a plan when you meet with God.

When I was a new believer, I came across a prayer notebook that helped me through those young years in the Lord. Later on, I began to use the Lord's Prayer as my personal plan for prayer. Over the years, I have followed many plans and have now developed one that I believe will help many of you, located in the appendix to this book. I will give you more details about this plan in chapter 16.

Just remember this: If you do not plan to pray, you will not pray. In order to be an effective prayer warrior, you need to plan to meet with God daily.

> Just remember this: If you do not plan to pray, you will not pray. In order to be an effective prayer warrior, you need to plan to meet with God daily.

Another guideline to follow in having a meaningful time with God daily is to actively engage in reading . . .

A Special Book

The special Book that you need to read is a compilation of sixty-six smaller books. This Book contains literally thousands of promises made to you from God Himself. This Book is so powerful that people have died for its message. It is not a Book written by man but a Book that is written by God. It was breathed into existence by a personal and perfect God. Therefore, it is a perfect Book.

This Book is called the Bible. The Bible is essential for your life. It needs to be studied. It needs to be memorized. It needs to be read daily.

There is no way that you can have a meaningful time with God without reading the Bible daily. The Bible is the main way God speaks to you. The Bible is His love letter to you. God's Word is intended to be a lamp for our feet and a light for our path. This kind of guidance is possible when you read it and study it during a daily time with Him.

Consider developing a plan for reading through God's Word. For years, I have used *The One Year Bible*. With this Bible, you will have a particular reading of God's Word every day, rather than flipping aimlessly through the Bible. Since you are very interested in having a meaningful time with God every day, strongly consider reading through God's Word on an annual basis.

Get involved in reading this special Book. Read it slowly. Your goal should not be to hurry through a chapter or a reading assignment but to hear God speak to you through the words of this Book. God's words in His book have the power to change your life. Let this special Book be a part of your daily time with God.

A Special Letter

On January 1, 1990, I began a spiritual discipline that has really impacted my personal walk with Christ. I have not missed one day in doing this spiritual practice. It has blessed me and touched my life in a powerful way.

At the conclusion of my time with God each day, the final thing I do is write a one-page letter to God. I begin the letter the same way every day by writing the words, "Dear God . . ." In this letter I try to do two things. First, I write down anything that I sense that God has specifically spoken to me about through His Word. Second, I write down the main things on my heart that I have prayed about during this time with God. Journaling is powerful because of the release that comes when you write down some of your greatest burdens and know you have given them to God.

This special letter that you write to God becomes the documentation of your spiritual life. If you take the time to read through these letters, you will discover God's activity that has been taking place in your life. It also reminds you of some special moments when you handed over some burdens to God.

Therefore, my walk with Christ has been documented daily since 1990. This means that I can go back and look at how God saw me through the challenges of Jeana's cancer, the challenges my children were facing, the challenges I was facing at my church, or just the challenges of life in general. Do you realize what this does? It increases your faith! Since you know God has seen you through before, you know that He will see you through again.

Consider developing the practice of writing a daily letter to God. You can use something as simple as a composition notebook or as sophisticated as a leather-bound journal. Just begin to write God a letter every day. In time, you will regard it as being one of the most dynamic things you have ever done in your spiritual growth plan.

A Special Goal

I have often heard that in order for something to become a habit in your life you have to do it for at least twenty-one days in a row. This is true whether the habit is a new diet, a new exercise plan, or a new spiritual discipline.

You should desire for your daily time with God to become a habit in your life. You do not want to live the rest of your Christian life with the inconsistencies of the past. The greatest habit you could ever establish in your life is to have a meaningful time with God daily.

Do you believe God is able to help you have a meaningful time with Him daily? Set a goal of meeting with God consistently for at least twenty-one days in a row. Mark your calendar. Do not let anything come before this in your life. God wants you to do it. He will enable you to keep your commitment. Begin it now, even while you are learning how to pray more effectively through this book. Remember, the number one priority in the life of a true disciple of Jesus Christ should be to have a meaningful time with God daily.

Set a goal of meeting with God for a specific amount of time every day. Always have a goal in mind. For example, if you read one chapter in God's Word, spent time in personal prayer through your plan to pray, and wrote a letter to God, how long would that take you? You are not on someone else's level right now—you are on your own level. Start there and grow!

Gene Layman

One of the finest laypersons I have ever met in my life is a man named Gene Layman. Gene is a private businessman who has an insatiable passion for God.

Each day, Gene rises early to meet with God. It is like clockwork to him. He prepares himself for the day, grabs his books, and heads out to a local restaurant to meet with God. You might think that a restaurant is not a very private place, but it is when you are there by 4:00 A.M. Gene goes to his special corner, where he pursues his relationship with the living God.

Many mornings, Gene has called me to tell me what God said to him that morning. Sometimes he wants to share a special word for me from his time with God. This word is never a harsh word of rebuke but a word of edification for me. His words are meant to build me up, and believe me, they have.

Gene Layman models these guidelines I have given to you in this chapter. If you could spend time with him, in a few short moments you would learn of his depth in his walk with Christ. For years and years, he has practiced what I have written about in this chapter. I guarantee that he would tell you today the same words I have already stated to you: The number one priority of a true disciple of Jesus is to have a meaningful time with God daily.

What It Will Do for You

When you pursue your relationship with God by having a meaningful time with Him daily, what will it do for you? I hesitate taking this approach because I detest the "consumer mentality" that is infiltrating the church. At the same time, I know that having a meaningful time with God daily will do some things for you that I definitely want you to know because of the potential impact on your life. The first thing this spiritual discipline can do for you is give you . . .

Spiritual Power

You cannot make it spiritually without a meaningful time with God daily. The fight is too ferocious, and you are too fragile. Your goal should not be simply to survive in this world, but to experience true spiritual victory over this world. Is this really possible? Yes, when you have a meaningful time with God daily.

> Why settle for what you can do when you can experience what God can do? His power flowing through your life gives you spiritual power for daily living.

Spiritual power is the result of having a meaningful time with God daily. God will use that time to fill you with His Spirit and His power. He will use that time to take back the control of your life from you. Why settle for what you can do when you can experience what God can do? His power flowing through your life gives you spiritual power for daily living.

Spiritual Direction

Have you ever wondered about God's will for your life? I am sure you have. One of the great benefits of a meaningful time with God daily is sensitivity to God's guidance for your life. He does not want you wandering around without His clear direction. He wants to make His will and His ways clear to you. This is discovered in a meaningful time with Him daily.

Spiritual Purpose

Few things are more important than having purpose for your life.

A lack of purpose has driven many people to hospitals and some to their graves. God wants to give His followers purpose.

When you have a meaningful time with God every day, you will begin to experience purpose for your life. You will discover that God wants to use you wherever you are in life. He wants to use you to make a difference with your life. He wants you to join Him in His purpose of seeing a lost, pagan world come into a dynamic relationship with Him.

His heart will become your heart. His purpose will become your purpose. When you have a meaningful time with God daily, He will give you true spiritual purpose for your life.

Back to the Basics

God's game plan for your life is discovered through having a meaningful time with Him. He is pursuing you. He wants a relationship with you. He wants you to fellowship with Him.

Experiencing a meaningful time with God is the most basic of the basics of Christianity. Just as football teams cannot win games while neglecting the basics of the game, Christians cannot experience God's work in their lives while neglecting the basic of having a meaningful time with God daily. It is the most fundamental part of the Christian life. Isn't it amazing how our enemy does all he can to keep us from doing this? Even Satan knows where the power is discovered in the Christian life.

If you genuinely desire to walk with God and to become a prayer warrior, then follow the guidelines I have given you about how to have a meaningful time with God daily. The time is short. It is past time for Jesus' disciples to get back to the basics. There are no shortcuts to spiritual victory. Stay with the fundamentals. When you do, the benefits will be innumerable and the blessings will be bountiful.

Section
Two

KEYS TO A POWERFUL
PRAYER LIFE

Chapter 4

How to Pray According to God's Will

The office facility that our church constructed in recent years has been a special workplace for our staff. When my office was being built, the designers asked what I wanted in my office. I requested only that the space allotted to me for ministering to people would remind me of God's purpose for my life and ministry. This was accomplished by printing the Great Commission of our Lord Jesus Christ on the walls of my office and placing a very large picture of the world behind my desk.

My office may be uniquely decorated, but in reality it is just like any other pastor's office. It contains some incredible memories. It also contains some very important information. Much of this information is confidential—no one needs to see it or know it other than me.

Due to the private information contained in my office, I hold one of the few keys to the office door. Although everyone is welcome to visit while I am in my office, the key is not given out to anyone who wants one. In fact, few persons have direct access to this office. Not any key will get you into my office; only the key uniquely designed for my office will give you access into this place.

Like the key that opens the door into my office, prayer is the key that unlocks the door to God's throne room. Would you like to have a key that unlocks the treasure chest of heaven? This treasure chest contains the powerful blessings that God created for you and wants to distribute to you. God's throne room is the place where you talk to God. It is the place where you offer your prayers to God and He answers them. Prayer is the key that unlocks the door to this treasure chest of heaven, God's throne room.

> God's throne room is the place where you talk to God. It is the place where you offer your prayers to God and He answers them.

In this special place, through your prayers, you get hold of God. In this special place, through your prayers, God gets hold of you. As a believer in Jesus Christ, you have the awesome privilege of experiencing the presence of God in this special place because the key of prayer gives you access to God. In this place, you pray. In this place, you offer praise. In this place, you worship. In this place, God changes you. Leaving this place, you are never the same.

I want the treasure chest of God made available to me. However, let me be honest with you about something. I do not seek the treasure chest of God; I seek God Himself. When I seek God first, I receive all that He wants me to have from His treasure chest. I receive the peace of His presence and the confidence of knowing that He is working in my life. In this secret place, God answers my prayers.

Prayer is a secret adventure. I like to refer to the experience of abiding in His presence through prayer as the secret place. One reason prayer seems difficult at times is because we have the challenge of bowing before the Lord in prayer in secret. No person may see us. Yet God sees us. And when we determine to pray, we do so because we are making a deliberate decision to depend upon the Lord rather than ourselves.

May I inform you of something that you may not know or may have forgotten? This treasure chest of God contains all the answers to your needs. In other words, even before you ask or know you have a need, your wonderful God has the supply. He has the answers to all of your prayers. Just think, prayer is the key that unlocks the door to God's throne room.

In this section I am going to share with you three keys to a powerful prayer life. If Jesus Christ is your Lord and Savior, you have all three of these keys. The result is that you can have a powerful prayer life. I have never met a Christian who does not want to have a powerful prayer life. I have heard hundreds of Christians say that they wished they could pray like this person or that person. The good news is that you do not have to go to a prayer conference to receive these keys. You already have each of these keys if you are a genuine follower of Jesus Christ.

Do you know why I am one of the only persons with a key to my office? Because I have the authority to access my office. Just like the key to my office represents my authority to enter that office, the keys I am going to give you in this section represent your authority to access God's throne room.

Would you file the next statement into your memory? **Prayer leads you to the power of God.** Jesus verified this when He said, "For Thine is the kingdom, and the power, and the glory, forever. Amen" (Matt. 6:13). Prayer is your immediate entrance into the power of God. God is power. Prayer is the means by which you communicate to God and He communicates to you.

Are you ready to enter into this treasure chest of God? Are you ready to enter into God's throne room? Are you ready to experience His power like never before? Are you ready to experience the confidence of God in your life by knowing He will answer your prayer? If you are ready to take your prayer life to a new level, let me inform you that the first key to entering God's throne room of prayer is for you to . . .

Pray According to God's Will

I am the father of two sons. These two teenagers are the joy of my life. The only time I ever have a challenge being a parent is when the will of one of my sons seems to be in conflict with my will. I can honestly tell you that this conflict does not occur much at all, because Josh and Nick are very mature. They have been trained from childhood that God's protection for them is discovered in walking in obedience to the will of their parents.

When Josh and Nick are earnestly seeking to know my will, they will ask me, "Dad, what do you think?" This question demonstrates their teachable spirit. If a situation they are facing has major significance in their lives, they will make sure that they know my desire about that situation. At times, if they are unsure that they want to line up under my will, they will attempt to escape the issue.

So many times, children get very frustrated when they cannot discern what their parents really want them to do. Many times, parents are very poor at relating their desires to their children because the parents really do not know their desires. Or they may be somewhat afraid of their children's response to those desires.

As a child of God, you should have a teachable spirit. You should desire to know the will of your Father in heaven—not simply in moments of crisis but at all times in all things. There are moments as a child of God that you may act like a teenager who is afraid to know your Father's will because you know He will not agree with your will. Can you relate to this?

One of the great comforts you can have as a child of God is that your Father in heaven does not operate with the same margin of error as human parents; in fact, He operates at a zero margin of error. He has a perfect plan for your life. He wants to share this plan with you daily and even momentarily. He never keeps His will from you because He is afraid of your reaction or rejection of it. He reveals it to you in His perfect timing. Count on this in relation to God's timetable: He is never too early or too late, but He is always on time. He knows what is best for you. He is ready to share with you what His will is for your life.

Prayer is the vehicle of communication by which you can understand God's will for your life more clearly. The challenge is that you have to learn to pray according to His will. First John 5:14–15 says, "This is the confidence which we have before Him, that, if we ask anything according to His will, He hears us. And if we know that He hears us in whatever we ask, we know that we have the requests which we have asked from Him." There is no need to come into prayer with a tentative nature. It is clear from these verses that you can enter God's throne room with confidence.

Confidence in prayer means that you can have freedom of speech in prayer. You can say anything to God you want to say. Confidence in prayer also means that you come to God and tell Him your needs. In other words, you can go to God anytime, anywhere, and about anything. Knowing this should give to you great confidence in prayer.

As you are praying, you are to pray about what *God* wants, not what *you* want. In fact, I am not sure God will give you an answer concerning some of your prayers until your will is totally surrendered to Him. The attitude that you should have is, "Lord, I am willing to receive Your will. If You want me to do it, I am ready. If You do not, then that is fine." At this point of self-denial, God brings into reality the heart of Jesus' prayer, "Not My will, but Thine be done" (Luke 22:42).

Therefore, your ultimate goal in prayer should be to pray according to what God wants for your life. God hears your prayers when you ask for the things that are in line with His will, His intention, and His desire for your life. Do you want God to hear your prayers? Do you ever wonder if He hears your prayers? The secret to God hearing your prayers is for you to ask for the things that are in line with His will. Passionate prayer will conform your will to the will of God. You can have the confidence that God hears you when you pray about the things that are in line with His will, and you can receive additional confidence, knowing that your requests will be met when they are asked according to His will.

God is a great and perfect Father. He wants to show you His will. He wants to meet all of your needs. Just as an obedient and teachable son will earnestly seek the will of his earthly father, as an obedient and teachable child of God you need to seek the will of your Father in heaven.

In relation to the truths discovered in 1 John 5:14–15, what is God saying to you? You can go to God anywhere, anytime, and about anything. When you go to God in prayer, you can freely express your heart with the words that He gives to you in prayer. There is no special formula to use in prayer, but the key is for you to pray about His desire for your life. When you go to God, talk to Him about His desire for your life, His desire for your family, His desire for your church, and His desire for your country. Use caution about always exploding with your intentions, or else you may forfeit God's activity in your life.

There is no special formula to use in prayer, but the key is for you to pray about His desire for your life.

The result of this kind of praying is that you will receive the confidence that you should have in prayer as you pray about what God wants in all situations, rather than what you might want. This kind of praying also results in your prayers being answered. Have you prayed according to God's will for your life? Have you prayed about God's will for your family? Have you prayed about God's will for your church? Have you prayed about God's will for your country? Since it is important to pray about God's will in these areas and others, there are three important questions I want to address in the remaining pages of this chapter. The first question is . . .

How Do You Know God's Will?

This is a very critical question. If God has promised that He will answer when you pray according to His will, then you should ask, "How do I know God's will?"

In the Bible, God reveals His will about all matters to you. If you are going to know God's will, then you are going to have to know the Scriptures. Learn to pray according to the Scriptures. Learn to search the Scriptures about the burden on your heart. See what God says about this burden, and then pray about your burden by using God's activity in the Scriptures. God has a unique way of speaking to you about "the matters of life" when you are reading through the Scriptures in a systematic manner. The breadth of life is covered in the breadth of the entire counsel of God. This is why it is important to read the entire Bible.

There are times when a major need comes into a person's life. For example, suppose you are a single adult in a dating relationship with someone, and things are getting rather interesting. You think about this person most of the time. When you are around this person, your heart flutters. The stars of love are in your eyes. If you have not gone to God yet about this relationship, then approach the Word of God and discover what God says about dating and marriage. Through your investigation of this subject in the Word, you are opening yourself up for God to speak to you. Through His Word, He will speak to you about this person. Pray about this person from God's point of view. Release the relationship in its entirety to God. Ask God for His will to take place, and in His time, He will either penetrate your heart with

His peace or saturate it with restlessness. Pray about what He wants you to do about that relationship.

When I pray, I often say to God, "Now, Lord, I have laid out several needs to You today. As I read Your Word now, if You so choose, speak to me about some of these needs." When I sense God is speaking to me through the Scriptures about one of these needs, I write the verse down beside the need and pray over it for a while. In His timing, God will confirm to me His will. The observation I have made through the years is that as I pray according to the Scriptures concerning this need, God conforms my will to His concrete direction concerning the need.

Sometimes I feel the bondage of sin taking hold of my life. Whenever I feel this pressure from the enemy or sense my own lack of repentance over this sin, I open my Bible to Psalm 51, where David confessed his sins before God. I read this psalm back to God, personalizing it for me and my sin. If you want to know the will of God, learn to personalize the Scriptures and pray them to God in relation to your need.

Sometimes Christians have a very poor view of God. They seem to think that God plays "hide-and-seek" with them concerning His will. God is a loving Father who wants you to know His will. He reveals His will in the Bible. I want to encourage you to follow this practice: Do not begin to pray seriously without this Book in your hand. Prayer and the Bible are like two wings on an airplane: You will not reach your destination without both of them. Your destination is discerning the will of God about all matters of life. The way you do this is through prayer and through the Bible.

By the way, the Father loves to hear His Word. Remind Him of what He said in it. Read it to Him. He loves to hear it! How do I know this? As a father of two sons, I love to hear my boys say to me, "You know, Dad, you said this. Therefore, Dad, you should do this." A loving father will not back away from his word to his children, and God never backs away from His Word to His children. The Bible is the most relevant book in the world today. God honors all of His words in this Book.

Are you praying according to God's will? I can tell you how you will answer this question by asking another question: Are you praying according to the Scriptures? If you are praying according to the Scriptures, you are praying according to God's will. Spend time in the Word of God. It will change your prayer life. It will change your thought life. It will change your life.

Another question I want to address about praying according to God's will is . . .

Do You Always Know God's Will?

There are times when you may not know God's will about a certain situation. This should not cause you to have a spiritual wreck. It should cause you to move with caution about the matter on your heart. The apostle Paul set a model of this for us. He told the church in Rome that he was "always in my prayers making request, if perhaps now at last by the will of God I may succeed in coming to you" (Rom. 1:10). Paul wanted to go to Rome. Several times he requested from the Father that he be permitted to go to Rome.

Notice the conditions Paul placed on his prayer. Let me paraphrase for you what I believe Paul was praying: "Lord, I have come to You several times about going to Rome. I really want to go, Lord. If You would grant me this request, I would sure appreciate it. Yet, I only want to go if You want me to go." Let me take it another step for you. He was saying to the Lord: "Lord, I do not want to go to Rome unless You really want me to go. I just pray You will let me go."

Be honest, do you ever pray like that? I do not believe there is anything wrong with praying like that because the emphasis is still on God's will, not your own, even though you may have a personal desire about the situation. Perhaps you are unsure about a job that you would like to have. Maybe you are interested in a promotion. Seek God's will about these matters. If He does not speak to you through His Word, then come to Him and pray, "Lord, I would really like to take this new job" or, "God, I would really like to take this new promotion." I do not think it is good to have trust in yourself in regard to prayer. Place all of your trust in God. So add these words to your prayer: "Lord, if it is not Your will for me to have this new job or this new promotion, take the desire away from me. If it is not Your will, keep the decision away from me."

If you truly want to seek God and His will, He will be faithful to make His will known to you. Through this process of seeking God's will, you learn the walk of faith.

In those times when you do not clearly understand God's will from His Word about a particular need or situation, do not hesitate to pray like Paul did. Just pray, "Lord, if You want me to . . . I will" or, "Lord, I would like to do this, but I only want to if You want me to do it." God will always honor a person who seeks Him with his or her whole heart.

Another question I want to address about this subject of praying according to God's will is . . .

Why Do You Need to Pray If God's Will Is Going to Be Done Anyway?

God is a sovereign God who is able to accomplish anything He chooses to accomplish. At the same time, you have a free will that at times may not be in conformity to God's will. Yet, God is able to engineer the circumstances in life to bring your will into conformity with His will. Knowing all of this, you still might ask, "Why should I pray if God's will is going to be done anyway?"

There are two reasons that you should pray. First, you should pray because God commanded for you to pray. He wants you to spend time with Him. God wants you to pray.

Another reason that you should pray is that God has chosen prayer as the means to meet your needs. Dependence upon God builds faith. When you see God respond to your requests, your trust in God is enlarged.

> Through prayer, God establishes a trust relationship with you and me. Our faith is enlarged when God's activity becomes evident in our lives. Therefore, prayer is an act of obeying God.

Prayer does not move God as much as it moves you toward God. It places you in a posture to receive what God has for your life. When you pray, God is more likely to meet your needs. His will is for you to talk to Him, abide in Him, and know that without Him you are nothing. This posture moves you into expecting God to do something in your life. Through prayer, God establishes a trust relationship with you and me. Our faith is enlarged when God's activity becomes evident in our lives. Therefore, prayer is an act of obeying God. This is why we should pray, even though we know God's will is going to be done.

A Spiritual Insight

God's Word clearly states that God wants you to pray. You pray for the purpose of communing with God, not for the purpose of getting something that you really want or think you need in your life. I want to share a spiritual insight with you that will bring this subject to an appropriate conclusion: **You are to pray, and God will determine when and how those prayers are answered.**

This may cause some problems from your perspective. You may struggle with the issue of when God answers your prayers. He never seems to move as quickly as you might desire. Remember: God alone is in charge of the timing of His answer to your prayers. Rest assured that God always answers your prayers. At times, He says yes. At other times, He says no. There are other times when His answer is, "Wait." God is in charge of the "when" of life, not you.

Another struggle you may face in prayer is how God may answer your prayer. It is impossible to see all God sees. There were times in your life when you really wanted God to answer your prayer in a certain way, but He did not do it. At that time, you were somewhat despondent about it. Yet when you look back at it now, you see that He was protecting you. He was caring for you when you did not know how to care for yourself.

When I was about to graduate from seminary, I preached at a church that wanted to call me as their pastor. It was a new church, located in the suburbs of a major metropolitan city in Texas. I dreamed of giving my entire life to that church.

When I preached in view of a call, everything went great. On the way back to the airport, the chairman of the pastoral search committee informed me that I needed to receive at least 95 percent of the vote for the church to call me. I was concerned because even Jesus Christ would do well to get that kind of vote in any church I have ever been in.

The church voted the next Sunday, and I received less than the required 95 percent vote. I was devastated. My ministry life was turned upside down. I became depressed about being rejected by this church and had difficulty staying focused on the church I was serving at the time.

In the course of time, God healed my heart and called me to the First Baptist Church in Palacios, Texas, one of my favorite church experiences of all time. The power of God fell on that place, and in three years the church tripled in attendance. God used that ministry to define me and prepare me for the future.

God protected me from what I had previously prayed for, initially thinking it was God's will. He then provided me a wonderful church that was truly in His will. As a result, I experienced the blessings of God that can only come when you trust and live in the providence of God.

It would be great to have 20-20 spiritual vision on the front side of certain situations, but that would take away the faith and the joy of the journey in prayer. No matter what your current situation, you can trust that God's will is always the best answer for your life, even if it's not the answer you expect at the time.

God wants you to pray. He will determine when and how your prayers are answered. The joy of the Lord is yours when you realize the reality of His protection in your life. He knows what is best for you, even when you do not know what is best for yourself.

Begin today to practice praying according to God's will. This key, given to you by the Master, will open up the treasure chest of God to you as you abide in that secret place, God's throne room. Enter into this special place by praying according to God's will.

Chapter 5 ■

HOW TO PRAY
IN JESUS' NAME

I am very grateful for the many doors of ministry God has opened up for me around the country. It is always a joy to go to another setting and relate God's truth with people. Even though I enjoy the privilege of ministry around the country, I do not enjoy the challenges of travel. The challenges of airlines and hotels seem to keep things interesting while I travel.

Security has become a big issue for the hotel industry. Many hotels have gone to the plastic entry card with the lock to the room coded on it. They will usually place this entry card into a brochure that has the number of your room on it and tell you something like this: "Do not lose this brochure because it has your room number on it. For security reasons, your room number is not displayed on your entry card."

Recently I arrived at a hotel and needed to check into my room before a meeting downstairs. I was already late due to my airline flight being delayed. I checked into the hotel, hurried to prepare for my meeting, and walked out of my room to attend the meeting in the hotel's conference room.

After a long meeting that went until late that night, I got on the elevator and went to the floor to go to my room for the evening. As I stepped out of the elevator, I reached into my pocket to get the entry card to my room. I had been successful in bringing the entry card, but in my hurried state I had failed to bring the brochure that had my room number on it. Therefore, the guessing game began.

I was really tired, and I did not want to go all the way downstairs again. So I tried to remember my room number. I thought I had done so; however, when I placed the entry card into the room that I supposed was mine, the code on the card did not activate the lock. I determined that I probably had the wrong room number. So I attempted to open another door. Again, the code did not activate the lock. At this point, frustration after a long day was setting in, so I hurried downstairs to the front desk. The clerk was busy checking in several people as well as answering the phone.

As I waited, my frustration increased. Finally, the clerk got to me. I told him my story, and then I had to be checked out, for security reasons, to make certain I was telling the truth. Approximately forty-five minutes after my initial attempt to get into my room, I received the correct room number. Not only did I not have the correct number to my room, but I was not even on the right floor when I tried to enter the two rooms!

When I finally got into my room that evening, I was relieved that my clothing was in the room I had been able to enter. At last, I was home for the evening. There is nothing like the joy of travel.

Do you ever wonder if the Lord has a sense of humor? One week after this experience, my wife and I went to spend the weekend in New York City. I was scheduled to preach for Jim Cymbala, pastor of the Brooklyn Tabernacle Church in Brooklyn, New York. When we arrived at the hotel and received the information about our room, I was determined not to forget my room number again. The Lord helped me to not forget it: I was assigned Room 666. Jeana and I laughed and proceeded to our room with the blessed assurance we would not forget our room number in that hotel.

One of the pivotal things I learned from my hotel experience is that the entry card, when coded correctly, will give you entry into your room. If the card has been coded incorrectly, the lock will not allow entry into the room. Even if the card is coded correctly, it is necessary to use it on the right door in order for successful entry to occur.

When you go to the Father in prayer, there is a code you can use that will give you immediate access into God's presence. This code is the name of Jesus.

When you go to the Father in prayer, there is a code you can use that will give you immediate access into God's presence. This code is never in error, and it will open all that God has for you when you enter into God's throne room. This code is the name of Jesus. When you use the name of Jesus in your prayer, you have access to all God has for you.

Pray in Jesus' Name

Those of us who have grown up in church life have had the privilege of experiencing some wonderful blessings of God. I have been very active in church my entire life. As a result, I have been mentored in prayer through the years by observing others' prayers in worship services and prayer meetings.

I remember in a very distinct way how people would pray in the church I attended most of my life. One of the normal prayers at my church sounded something like the following:

Dear Father, We are grateful for this day. We thank You for the blessings of our life. We thank You for the blessing of our family. Now, Lord, be with our pastor today as he preaches. In Jesus' name, amen.

This generalized praying probably did not grab the horns of the altar, but there is something that I will never forget about all the prayers in that small church. Every person I ever heard pray in that church would conclude their prayer by saying, "In Jesus' name, amen." I am confident that most people probably did not know what that phrase meant but just prayed it out of habit.

What does it mean to pray in Jesus' name? Just before Jesus went to the cross to die for your sins, He had a very important conversation with His closest followers. In the sixteenth chapter of the Gospel of John, Jesus spoke about the relationship the Holy Spirit would have with His disciples. Jesus instructed His disciples about the role of the Holy Spirit in prayer. In verses 23 and 24, Jesus said, "Truly, truly, I say to you, if you shall ask the Father for anything, He will give it to you in My name. Until now you have asked for nothing in My name; ask, and you will receive, that your joy may be made full." Jesus gave His disciples a key to a powerful prayer life. That key is to make all requests known to the Father in Jesus' name.

Jesus encouraged you to ask the Father for anything. When you go to the Father in prayer, you are not going to your buddy. You are not going to the man upstairs. You are going to the King of Kings and the Lord of Lords. Jesus has given you the privilege to go to His Father and ask Him for anything. The word *ask* depicts the image of requesting something from someone who is your superior. The Father is your superior. You cannot simply yank His chain and "name it and claim it." You need to understand who God is, live under His authority, and receive His will for your life as you make your requests known to Him in Jesus' name. When you ask the Father for something "in Jesus' name," you need to understand that this phrase is neither a magical formula that attempts to bargain with God nor a vain repetition.

In this section of the book, I am giving you three keys to a powerful prayer life. In the previous chapter, you read about the first key: praying according to God's will. In this chapter, you are reading about the second key: praying in Jesus' name. Since praying in Jesus' name is the code for us to enter God's throne room, I want to address the question of . . .

Why Should You Pray in Jesus' Name?

There are many reasons why you should pray in Jesus' name. I want to highlight just three of these reasons. The first reason is . . .

Jesus' Name Is the Gateway to God

In the city of St. Louis, Missouri, a large white arch called the "Gateway to the West" stands in the heart of downtown. This arch symbolizes that the city of St. Louis is the gateway to the West—the city where you enter the western part of the United States.

A gateway is an entry point. Jesus' name is the entry point into the presence of God. It is the code of entry into God's throne room. Coming to the Father in Jesus' name gives you the assurance of being able to approach God.

You cannot approach God in your own name. You cannot approach God in your own ability. You can approach God only in the name of Jesus Christ. He is the gateway, the entry point, into the presence of God. This initial entry point takes place at your salvation experience. In John 14:6, Jesus says, "I am the way, and the truth, and the life; no one comes to the Father, but through Me."

The Bible teaches that Jesus is the only way to have a personal relationship with God. Jesus regarded Himself as the only way to God. He said He is the only truth. There is no truth apart from Him. He also understood that He is the only One who can grant spiritual life. Jesus is the gateway to God!

If you are going to do serious business with God, then you must pray in the name above all names—the name of Jesus. An example of this would be:

> Father, I do not come to You today in my own name or my own ability. I do not even have a right to talk to You except by and through the person of Jesus Christ. I approach You, but not in my own name or my own ability. Father, I approach You in the strong and powerful name of Jesus Christ. Amen.

When you pray in Jesus' name as illustrated for you here, you have punched the code. You have used the key that will get you into God's presence.

The first reason you should pray in Jesus' name is because His name is the entry point, the gateway to God. His name gives you access into the presence of God, where you can do some serious communication with God. Another reason you should pray in Jesus' name is . . .

It Reminds the Father of Jesus

I tend to live a very hurried life. The schedule I keep is very busy, but if you want to stop me for a moment, all you have to do is talk to me about my sons, Josh and Nick. I will immediately stop and talk about either one of my boys. The mere mention of either of their names brings everything else to a halt for a few moments, and you will have my immediate attention. If you have a few good things to say about them, I can add to those with a whole lot of other good things. As a father, I love to be reminded of my two sons.

When you go to the Father in prayer, mention the name of His Son, Jesus. He loves that name. He is reminded of His Son and all He has done every time you mention Jesus' name. Whenever God hears Jesus' name, He is reminded of being one with Him. He is reminded of the preexistence of His Son. He is reminded of how Jesus substituted Himself to die for your sins. He is reminded of how Jesus is at His right hand right now and lives to make intercession for you. Therefore, anytime I pray in Jesus' name, I am reminding the Father of all of these things and more about His Son, Jesus Christ.

Let me give you an example of this truth about reminding the Father of His Son, Jesus Christ, in prayer:

> Father, thank You for letting me come to You and talk to You today. Thank You for the privilege of letting my requests be made known to You in Jesus' name. I lay my life and these requests before You in the name of Your wonderful and beloved Son, Jesus Christ. Amen.

When the Father hears you pray something like these words, He says, "Yes! My Son is wonderful and He is My beloved!" By using the name of Jesus Christ in prayer, you are reminding the Father of His Son and all His Son has done. At the mere mention of Jesus' name, you get the immediate attention of the Father.

Another reason why you should pray in Jesus' name is . . .

Jesus' Name Is Your Authority to Tie Your Request to the Father's Will

The name of Jesus is the most powerful name in heaven and on earth. Any time you take a request to God the Father in Jesus' name, you are tying it to the most authoritative name that has ever been given anywhere in the world. This means that you are taking your requests to God with authority.

Much of the time, prayer is uncertain ground for many believers. By observing the tentative nature of many Christians, you might think the ground is filled with more land mines than blessings. This is not the kind of praying I am writing about here. You should not feel as if you are walking on eggshells with God. You should sense you are walking with the authority of His Son, Jesus.

> Any time you take a request to God
> the Father in Jesus' name, you are tying it to
> the most authoritative name that has ever
> been given anywhere in the world.

By offering your request to the Father in Jesus' name, you are tying your request with great authority. The Father loves Jesus' name. Offering your requests in Jesus' name gains the Father's attention. By tying your requests to Jesus' name, you are submitting to the will of God about each request. Remember, it is not "My kingdom come and my will be done"; it is "Thy kingdom come" and "Thy will be done, on earth as it is in heaven" (Matt. 6:10).

For example, let's imagine for a moment that you have a child who has drifted away from God. This child's departure from God's life has worn you down. How should you pray about this?

> Lord, my heart is broken over my child. He is away from You and
> the way he has been raised in his life. I just come to You today in
> the strong name of Jesus, asking for Your authority to take place
> in that situation. In Jesus' name, reign in this situation. Amen.

When you pray in this way, you are submitting your will to God's will about this situation. You are tying your request in an authoritative manner to the Lord Jesus Christ. You are asking God to do a miracle in your child's life.

Concerning this critical need, can God do a miracle? Absolutely! God can always do a miracle. The greater question is whether it is God's will to do a miracle in this child's life. When you tie your requests to the name of Jesus Christ, you offer them to God with authority. At this point, God becomes personally involved in the situation.

Pray Specifically, Not Generally

I want to encourage you to get out of the generalities of prayer. Stop praying in a general way. Stop offering general requests before God. Generalities are portrayed in prayer with statements like, "Thank You for all things" or, "Bless me with everything." Get away from this kind of praying. This will not lead to a powerful prayer life.

When I was in college, a professor told my preaching class that he did not appreciate "GWOT" sermons. He defined "GWOT" sermons as sermons that were about "God, the World, and Other Things." He was gently rebuking our class for preaching in generalities. The end result of that kind of preaching is that no one will understand what the preacher is trying to say.

Much prayer that is done today is "GWOT" praying. Our praying is so general at times, it is as though we are praying for "God, the World, and Other Things." Do not pray like this. Get away from the generalities.

When you begin to pray about specific requests and tie them one by one to the authoritative name of Jesus Christ, God is drawn to you quickly. He wants to know your heart. His specific interest in you and His interest in your specific prayer requests prove that God wants a personal relationship with you. This relationship is developed through practicing effective prayer principles. God will answer specific prayers that are directed to Him and linked with the authoritative name of Jesus.

A Closing Word

I cannot write a chapter about the importance of praying in Jesus' name without sharing a climactic passage with you from God's Word.

Since praying in Jesus' name is a key to a powerful prayer life, His name must be very powerful. Philippians 2:9–11 proclaims, "Therefore also God highly exalted [Jesus], and bestowed on Him the name which is above every name, that at the name of Jesus every knee should bow, of those who are in heaven, and on earth, and under the earth, and that every tongue should confess that Jesus Christ is Lord, to the glory of God the Father."

This passage is such a dynamic word about the name of Jesus Christ. The name of Jesus is the name above every name. His name is better than any other name. His name stands for Savior. His name stands for purity, righteousness, and holiness. There is no blemish at all in the name of Jesus. His name is perfect. His name is powerful!

One day each knee on this earth will bow out of honor and respect for your Savior, Jesus Christ. It may not be cool in today's church to be on your face before God; however, one day you will be on your face before God every time the name of Jesus is mentioned. Even the demons in hell will bow at the mention of the name of Jesus. Why? Because they know that Jesus is Lord.

You cannot get to God on your own merit. You cannot pray to God in your own name. You cannot bribe God to answer your requests. There is no need for any of these things because God has given you the key to a powerful prayer life.

This key to a powerful prayer life is praying in Jesus' name. By praying in Jesus' name, you enter into the very presence of God. By praying in Jesus' name, you remind the Father of all that Jesus has done. By praying in Jesus' name, you link your requests to the Father for His will to take place and His authority to occur in every situation.

You will never go wrong when you link your prayer requests to the most powerful name under all of heaven, the name of Jesus. You know, there really is something about that name!

Chapter 6 ■

HOW TO PRAY
IN THE SPIRIT

Imagine for a moment that you are alone in a very quiet and beautiful place. While sitting at a table, you look out the window at the beautiful mountain range that surrounds you. As you look down on the table, you see a blank piece of paper and a writing pen. Your assignment is to write on that blank sheet of paper all that you know about the subject of praying in the Spirit. What would you write on the paper? Would you even know enough to fill the blank sheet?

I have often wondered what the results would be if I led a congregation on a Sunday morning in this exercise. There is no question that many people would turn in a blank sheet of paper. Beyond that, I am confident that a variety of answers would be erroneous. Few answers would be on target about the subject.

I am disturbed how a biblical truth like praying in the Spirit is treated by some Christians. Many Christians never even discuss this subject; they just ignore it. Others look at it as a fanatical teaching that is practiced only by those who are too emotional about their faith. Since they equate praying in the Spirit with extremism, they do not want to have anything to do with it. Others abuse the phrase "praying in the Spirit" by saying it is something that it is really not. The result of this mistreatment is that ignorance and confusion abound on an essential teaching of the Christian life.

A Man Named Jude

Jude was the half brother of Jesus Christ. Even though he could have boasted about his relationship to Jesus, Jude instead referred to himself as a "slave of Jesus Christ." Jude was a man for his times. He was very concerned about his culture and burdened that the godless culture in which he was living was invading the church.

Jude intended to write a letter to Christians that instructed them on the basics of salvation and the Christian life. However, Jude received word that false teachers were invading the church with counterfeit teachings. These false teachers were twisting the truth of the grace of God and making it appear as a license to sin. Jude was startled that this false teaching was so rampant and yet no one was addressing it. He knew that someone needed to stand against these false teachers and their wrong teachings so the church of Jesus Christ would not tolerate their poor doctrine.

This courageous leader named Jude stood for Christ. He contended for the faith just like an athlete agonizes to cross the finish line, stretching every nerve and muscle to that mark of completion. Jude's defense of the faith was an experience of agony that demonstrates to everyone that defending the faith may be costly.

This courageous leader named Jude stood for Christ. He contended for the faith just like an athlete agonizes to cross the finish line, stretching every nerve and muscle to that mark of completion.

The faith that Jude defended was the faith that kept him. He knew that God would protect him and guard him as he did what was right. Jude had this kind of courage because of his commitment to biblical truth and to prayer. In the twentieth verse of his letter to these Christians, Jude writes, "But you, beloved, [are] building yourselves up on your most holy faith; praying in the Holy Spirit." What does this scripture mean?

The "most holy faith" mentioned in this verse refers to the doctrines and the teachings of God's Word. Faith cannot be holy without the Word of God. Faith does not even exist without the Word of God. Remember that Jude was calling for Christians to contend for the faith. In this verse he is saying that believers are built up on the concrete truth of God's Word.

If Jude lived in our culture today, he would be a very unusual Christian. The reason for this is because he had . . .

A Most Holy Balance

Jude was not a wild-eyed, religious radical but a man of God who was theologically balanced. He was a man who not only understood the importance of truth and faith but also the power of prayer. In fact, he understood prayer in a unique way: He understood how prayer relates to the Holy Spirit. This is why he instructed Christians to pray "in the Holy Spirit." Praying in the Spirit is one of the keys to a powerful prayer life.

Notice the balance in verse 20. As a Christian, you are to be built up in the most holy faith, and at the same time, you are to pray in the Spirit. When you pursue the Word of God, you pursue a relationship with the Holy Spirit. When you pursue a relationship with the Holy Spirit, you will pursue the Word of God. The Holy Spirit will always point you to Jesus Christ and lead you to the Word of God. When you know the Word of God, you are equipped to pray in the Spirit.

Effective prayer cannot be accomplished without knowing, believing, and practicing God's Word. It is more important for you to know what God says to you than for you simply to say things to God. What you say to God in prayer will be determined by what God says to you in His Word.

If you will implement the truths of the twentieth verse in Jude's book, you will achieve this "most holy balance." You will join the Word of God with your relationship to the Holy Spirit. How balanced are you at these two truths in your life? Do you lean to one of them and ignore the other? If you lean to God's Word without a personal relationship with the Holy Spirit in prayer, you will have knowledge with no life. If you lean to a personal relationship with the Holy Spirit without an understanding of God's Word, you will have an appearance of life with no spiritual depth.

I want to make two observations about our need to have this most holy balance. The first observation is . . .

When You Have the Word and Little Prayer, You Have Some Spiritual Light but No Spiritual Power

Most Christians who take the time to read books like this one have some commitment to the Word of God. Usually, their commitment is much stronger to the Word of God than to a relationship with the Holy Spirit of God. You may understand what the Bible is saying, but if the Holy Spirit is not moving mightily in your life, you will have little spiritual power. If the Holy Spirit is not empowering you daily, you cannot teach, preach, witness, or communicate God's Word in a way that will capture the attention of this generation.

Your challenge is to grow in your knowledge of the Word of God and in your relationship with the Holy Spirit. Maybe you can teach good lessons from God's Word. Perhaps you can even preach good sermons from God's Word. Yet, when you allow the Holy Spirit to accompany you as you communicate God's truth, you will capture the attention of your generation. Your goal should not be just to have spiritual light but to have spiritual light accompanied with spiritual power. Only a balance of the Word of God and the ministry of prayer will bring about this holy balance.

The second observation about this most holy balance is . . .

When You Have Prayer and Not Much of the Word, You Have Spiritual Zeal but No Knowledge

This imbalance is so dangerous. People who live in this spiritual imbalance think they have spiritual life, but in reality they only have simple enthusiasm. Spiritual zeal is meaningless if it is not built up by the Word of God.

The way this dangerous extremism occurs is that some people do not balance reading the Word and praying in the Spirit. If all you have is spiritual zeal, without having a commitment to being built up by God's Word daily, then you have dangerous extremism. Spiritual prayer must be blended with biblical knowledge in order for you to have spiritual power, rather than meaningless zeal.

Your goal in your spiritual life should not be merely acquiring information or achieving a powerful experience. Your goal in your spiritual life should be spiritual transformation. This takes a personal relationship with the Holy Spirit combined with a growing understanding of God's Word. Accomplishing this most holy balance will cause you to grow in your Christian life.

As a Christian, you have the privilege of entering God's throne room, where you can receive numerous blessings from God's treasure chest. One key that will get you into this special place of prayer is praying according to God's will. The second key that will open this special place for you is praying in Jesus' name. The third key is praying in the Holy Spirit. Each of these keys will give you a powerful prayer life. I want to investigate what it means for you to pray in the Holy Spirit. In order to do this, I first want to share with you . . .

What It Does Not Mean to Pray in the Spirit

I want to make sure that you interpret what it means to pray in the Holy Spirit in the context of what Jude wrote in his letter to Christians. I want to challenge you not to interpret this through your personal experience or through your religious tradition. These are not your authority for what you believe or practice—the Bible alone is your authority. Looking again at this letter from Jude, let's interpret what Jude is *not* saying about praying in the Holy Spirit.

Praying in the Holy Spirit Does Not Mean You Pray in Tongues

There is no indication whatsoever that praying in the Holy Spirit refers to praying in tongues. In fact, Jude doesn't even mention the gift of tongues in his letter.

The gift of tongues (or languages) is a spiritual gift that was demonstrated on the Day of Pentecost. As people gathered in Jerusalem from all over the world for the Feast of Pentecost, God sent His Spirit upon the Christians in Jerusalem. They began to speak in languages they did not know but that others knew. They spoke in these languages for the purpose of sharing the gospel of Jesus Christ. The result was that at least three thousand people came to Christ. The emphasis was not the phenomenon of the gifts of tongues; the miracle was that God provided a way for all people gathered for the Feast of Pentecost to be able to hear the gospel of Jesus Christ in their own language. I believe it is important that there is no reference to praying in the Spirit in Acts 2, where this experience is recorded.

In 1 Corinthians chapters 12 and 14, the apostle Paul's references to the gift of tongues do not refer to praying in the Holy Spirit. In fact, the tongues mentioned in 1 Corinthians were causing problems in public worship. The Corinthians were rebuked for attempting to duplicate the tongues of Acts 2 by the works of the flesh and given specific guidelines on how they were to worship.

I mention these passages because it is important that persons do not put their theology together like a jigsaw puzzle. When you piece together a puzzle, you will attempt a great deal of "trial and error." But God doesn't work like that. He spoke His truth about praying in the Holy Spirit in the same verse that He spoke of being built up by the Word of God. God knows the need for balance. He knows the tendency of believers to run after an emotional experience without having the foundation of God's Word.

Praying in the Holy Spirit is a biblical truth. We cannot let the extremism of some, the misinterpretation of others, or the deadness of a few negate the truth of praying in the Holy Spirit. We cannot let others and their preferences rob us of one of God's wonderful truths. Let's permit this truth to stand on its own as mentioned by Jude. Praying in the Spirit does not mean that you pray in tongues.

Another thing that Jude was clear about was that . . .

Praying in the Spirit Does Not Mean You Pray in a Prayer Language

There is no indication at all in this passage or other passages in the Scripture that praying in the Spirit has anything to do with praying in a special prayer language. Some Christians claim that they have a private prayer language. Some of those people would say this is what it means to pray in the Spirit. I do not believe that praying in the Spirit has anything to do with praying in a private prayer language. In fact, I have studied this subject in depth. Critical study of the biblical texts and of the original languages does not verify a prayer language in the Scriptures.

> I do not believe that praying in the Spirit has anything to do with praying in a private prayer language.

Therefore, those who proclaim they have a prayer language cannot use Jude's letter to justify this practice. For those who want to investigate this truth of praying in the Spirit, do not disqualify the truth based on others who may try to equate it with the gift of tongues or the ability to have a prayer language. Let the Word of God be the Word of God. Let the truth of praying in the Spirit stand on its own.

What It Means to Pray in the Spirit

In our search for truth, I want us to continue investigating what it means to pray in the Holy Spirit. Praying in the Holy Spirit means that you . . .

Pray According to the Leadership of the Spirit

When you pray, do you pray under the leadership of the Holy Spirit? Do you run through a prayer agenda without considering the Spirit's guidance in your time of prayer? When you pray under the Spirit's leadership, you cannot be in a hurry. If you are in a rush, you cannot pray under the Spirit's leadership. How can you begin to pray according to the leadership of the Holy Spirit?

You begin with moments of not saying anything. Meditate on the things of God. I would encourage you to begin by praying something like, "Lord, I come to You in the name of Jesus today. I do not want to have moments of vain repetition that will not please You, but I want You to show me what to pray for right now." It is important to have a plan to pray. If you don't already have such a plan, I will provide one for you in the last chapter of this book. Yet, whatever your plan is, you need to have enough flexibility to let the Holy Spirit lead you in your prayer time. A plan should be used to give you a general direction, not to place you into bondage as you pray.

When you pray under the leadership of the Holy Spirit, He will lead you to pray by the Word of God. At times, I have had some people say to me, "Pastor, I am praying about getting a divorce, and I really sense the Holy Spirit is leading me to do so." The Bible is very clear about divorce: God does not like it. The Holy Spirit will always lead you to fulfill the Word of God. Therefore, the Spirit will not lead you to be divorced if Scripture does not permit it to take place. You cannot let the phrase "the Spirit is leading me" become a means to justify an action that is contrary to God's Word.

Praying under the leadership of the Spirit means that you will pray by and with the Word of God. When you pray under the leadership of the Holy Spirit, you will let God show you what you need to pray for and about in your time of prayer. God will show you what to pray for. Listen to Him. Let His Spirit talk to your spirit. At times, just be quiet and let God lead you.

Praying in the Holy Spirit also means that you . . .

Pray with Assistance from the Holy Spirit

Years ago, I followed the green and gold of Baylor University football. While I was a pastor in Texas, I traveled with a family in my church to several Baylor Bear football games. I will never forget going to Texas A&M University's Kyle Field to watch the Bears play the Texas Aggies. It was a memorable experience. I have also seen Aggie football on national television several times, and I assure you, there is nothing like it. The crowd at Aggieland is known as the Twelfth Man. They stand the entire ball game, symbolizing that they support their team and are ready to suit up for the game if they are needed. They hunch over and yell for their team at the top of their voices. They sway from right to left to the music of the dynamic Aggie band. They kiss the lady next to them every time the team scores a touchdown. What a great tradition!

The eleven Texas Aggies on the field are not by themselves. They are supported and assisted by thousands and thousands of Texas Aggie fans. Whoever goes onto Kyle Field to play the Aggies goes on with a great disadvantage. Just as the fans of Aggieland assist the players, the Holy Spirit assists you in prayer. As the fans of Texas A&M football push their team to victory, the Holy Spirit pulls you toward God and to spiritual victory. Romans 8:26 says, "And in the same way the Spirit also helps our weakness; for we do not know how to pray as we should, but the Spirit Himself intercedes for us with groanings too deep for words."

There are times in the Christian life when you do not know how to pray. This passage is very clear that God is not talking about groanings with words or in a prayer language. This passage is speaking of how the Holy Spirit comes to assist you in prayer when you do not know what to pray. The Holy Spirit is praying for you to have victory. He is praying for you to fulfill God's will in your life. He is praying for you to have assistance from Him.

When you pray with assistance from the Holy Spirit, your prayer will be something like this: "Lord, I do not know how to pray about this matter. I must have Your help. I must have Your assistance. As You lead me to pray about this, may Your Spirit utter to the Father what the depths of my heart feel about this matter. Assist me, Holy Spirit, right now as I pray."

Praying in the Holy Spirit is letting the Spirit assist you in your time of prayer. Praying in the Spirit also means to . . .

Pray with Power from the Spirit

In October 1997, more than one million men filled the Washington, D.C., Mall to beseech God to send revival to America. This event, called Stand in the Gap, was a great moment in the history of American Christianity. In fact, it could have been the largest gathering of Christians in the history of the world.

I was asked to speak during the program. On the evening prior to this significant event, the speakers and participants gathered together in a prayer meeting. The power of God came upon the meeting as we prayed for one another. As we laid hands on various people, the power of God was ushered into that place. We prayed with true spiritual power.

One of the reasons Stand in the Gap was so powerful in the lives of many Christians was that the power of God first fell upon the leadership. The power of God in prayer usually precedes the power of God demonstrated in a public meeting.

> One of the reasons Stand in the Gap was so powerful in the lives of many Christians was that the power of God first fell upon the leadership.

Prayer leads you to the power of God, both in personal times of prayer and in public meetings of believers. God is attracted to men and women who want to pray in the Spirit. He will bless those who will pray in the Spirit with power.

Prayerlessness means you are depending on yourself. Prayer in the Spirit means that you are depending on God. When you depend on God, you will receive His power when you pray.

When His power comes upon you, mighty things begin to happen. You begin to experience power from on high. You begin to pray for things you did not have a burden to pray for before this time. You are energized, filled, and empowered by His Spirit. You are granted the authority of Jesus Christ. You will experience boldness, courage, and faith like never before. It is a faith-building moment. A powerful moment. A true God moment! When you are praying in the Spirit, experiencing His power, you become God's tool. At times, you are simply a vessel in the hand of God as you represent His people and their needs before God. Yes, prayer leads you to the power of God.

The Chalk Talk

It is a great experience to be in a locker room just before kickoff and hear the final talk given by the coach. This is called the coach's final "chalk talk." He goes over the final details. You faintly hear the bands playing and the fans yelling. You are trying to focus on the final details the coach is giving you. His final words are words of motivation to you.

Moments before He ascended into heaven to be with the Father, Jesus gathered His disciples for a final chalk talk. He gathered them together in Jerusalem and shared with them that the Holy Spirit would soon come upon them. He stated that they would be endowed with God's power from on high.

His disciples did not respond with, "We do not want that" or, "Oh, that sounds charismatic." No, they were in tune with what Jesus was saying. He told the disciples that the power they would receive would be their power to let everyone in the world know that He died for their sins and rose again to show His sacrifice was accepted by the Father.

In this Spirit talk, Jesus was preparing His disciples to pray in the Holy Spirit. He was preparing them to enter into real God power in their lives. This is why Paul wrote in Ephesians 6:18: "With all prayer and petition, pray at all times in the Spirit." Paul knew that the wardrobe of the believer had to be empowered by praying in the Spirit. Real warriors are prayer warriors! Prayer warriors are people who know the importance of praying in the Spirit at all times—praying under His leadership, praying with His assistance, and praying in His power. This is what it truly means to pray in the Spirit.

These Three Keys

In this section, I have given you the three keys to a powerful prayer life. I hope your appetite has increased to be a real prayer warrior. You cannot become a true prayer warrior without using these keys.

Remember, God's throne room is that special place where you experience the presence of God and all God has for you. The three keys for you to access God's throne room are:

• Pray According to God's Will
• Pray in Jesus' Name
• Pray in the Spirit

These three keys will lead you into greatness with God. They will unlock the chest that contains the fullness of God's blessings.

As you practice praying in the Holy Spirit, pray according to the leadership of the Holy Spirit in your life. Practice praying with the Holy Spirit's assistance in your life. Practice praying with power from the Holy Spirit. When you begin to pray like this, you will pray with power like never before.

Now that you understand these things, you are prepared to go to a new level in your prayer life. Join me as, in the following pages, we embark on a journey, headed for a new level of prayer.

Section
Three

MOVING TO A NEW
LEVEL IN PRAYER

Chapter 7 ■

HOW TO CALL
UPON THE LORD

I t was a defining spiritual day in our lives. On a hot, summer Sunday morning, Jeana and I departed from our hotel and traveled into the city of Brooklyn, New York. Our tour guides were a humble and modest couple who had been believers in Jesus Christ for only a few short years. Their excitement and servant hearts captivated our attention as we chatted on the drive.

Coming into Brooklyn, we saw numerous buildings. Finally, we slowed down, and I noticed a great number of people walking away from one particular building. Lined up beside the hundreds of people exiting the building was a crowd of people wanting to go into the building. No, they were not standing in line to attend a Broadway show. The people were leaving and preparing to enter one of America's great and unique churches, the Brooklyn Tabernacle Church.

You may have heard their music or seen their story on national television. Located in the heart of downtown Brooklyn, the Brooklyn Tabernacle Church is one of the miracle stories of Jesus Christ today. Years ago, this church could barely operate, but then the wind of God's Spirit began to blow. Now the church stands as one of the greatest testimonies to Jesus Christ in all of the world.

I was asked by the senior pastor, Jim Cymbala, to spend a Sunday ministering to his people. At the time I was there, they had four services taking place each Sunday. Each service lasted at least two hours. Pastor Cymbala had asked me to preach two of the services: at 12:00 noon and 7:30 P.M. We left the hotel at 10:30 A.M. and returned just before midnight.

This was not McChurch, where you drive in and drive out to have your most prominent "felt need" met for the day, preferably in a one-hour time limit. This was not Suburban Church USA, where a beautiful campus existed on one hundred acres of land and offered the best of the best to all who attend. This was not even Boomerville Church in Hotshot America, where only the executives and the affluent of the region attend. It was not Big-Time Church either, where Dr. Wonderful is the celebrity pastor who walks in and around his people like a movie star.

When the Brooklyn Tabernacle Church gathers for worship, they are there to meet God in His timing, regardless of how long it takes.

When the Brooklyn Tabernacle Church gathers for worship, they are there to meet God in His timing, regardless of how long it takes. Their campus will probably not appear on the cover of a Christian magazine as the place every Christian must see. It is a church for all people. People of various colors and nationalities, as well as poor people and some who appear to have sufficient means to live a good life in metropolitan New York, attend the weekly worship services. Convenience is not even an issue because most come to the church not by car, but by subway. Their pastor is not like Dr. Wonderful in most churches today, who thinks he is a little bit better than everyone else. Pastor Jim Cymbala is a real servant. He walks slowly among the people, praying and touching people with his genuine Christian life.

This church knows how to worship. Their pastor leads them to meet God weekly. In each of these four services, three of which I witnessed, he offered leadership in prayer, ministry, and music. He spent the entire day expending himself for the sake of the gospel. In the one service I attended but did not preach, Pastor Cymbala expounded the Word like a true shepherd. It was not a simple sermonette, but a strong biblical message that was true to the text in every way.

When the people prayed that Sunday, they did not have a stiff and dignified time when the pastor prayed in the king's English. It was a time when all of God's people poured their hearts out toward God and called out to the Lord in a literal manner. It was not, "Hush, hush, do not disturb anyone else." It was a loud and noisy moment that was signified by genuine brokenness and prayer. Yes, the people of this church called out to the Lord to meet them on that day. I have to admit that I was a little taken aback by it, not because it bothered me but because I was surprised that a growing church like this had such openness in worship and prayer.

In his book, *Fresh Wind, Fresh Fire,* Jim Cymbala recounts the story of how God turned this church upside down. He is careful not to attribute this turning to a church growth method but to the Lord, who gave the church fresh spiritual wind and real spiritual fire. This is an exciting book that every believer needs to read, especially those who are sick and tired of boring church and are ready to have church God's way.

The secret of the Brooklyn Tabernacle Church is its ministry of prayer. On Tuesday evenings, the worship center overflows with people who come for the purpose of prayer. Deep, genuine prayer goes on each Tuesday evening. In *Fresh Wind, Fresh Fire,* Cymbala writes:

> The Bible [says], "My house shall be called a house of prayer for all nations." Preaching, music, the reading of the Word—these things are fine; I believe in and practice all of them. But they

must never override prayer as the defining mark of God's dwelling. The honest truth is that I have seen God do more in people's lives during ten minutes of real prayer than in ten of my sermons. . . . Have you ever noticed that Jesus launched the Christian church, not while someone was preaching, but while people were praying? . . . Am I the only one who gets embarrassed when religious leaders in America talk about having prayer in public schools? We don't have even that much prayer in many churches.[1]

Prayer is not confined to Tuesday evenings at the Brooklyn Tabernacle. Each worship service is filled with deep, abiding, serious prayer that exudes what the Scriptures tell us about calling upon the Lord in prayer.

By the time we returned to our hotel that evening, Jeana and I had experienced serious church led by a focused man of God. Pastor Cymbala stayed until the end, involved in continual encouragement and personal ministry to others. It was refreshing to be a part of something that is so reminiscent of the New Testament church. I would like for every young pastor, every seminary student, and every seeking Christian to experience what I experienced that Sunday, not just on the front lines in a public worship service but even behind the scenes. Nothing plastic. Nothing counterfeit. Just real Christianity.

What I witnessed that Sunday was a church operating on a different spiritual level from most. The works of the flesh were not manifested, only the works of the Spirit of God. It was truly refreshing! This work of the Spirit has taken this church to a new spiritual level because of its emphasis on prayer. This church really knows how to pray. It knows what it means biblically and practically to call upon the Lord. If you are a skeptic or a cynic, I would remind you of one thing: This church has not been raised up on the side of an interstate, on one hundred acres of land, or in a region overflowing with an exciting population explosion. This church stands as a testimony in downtown Brooklyn, as a spiritual tower of God's power! And I believe this amazing growth is all because of the grace of God and the prayers of His people.

Are you ready to go to a new level in your prayer life? Are you ready to leave Church Usual and experience Church Unusual? Are you aware of what you need to know to go to a new level in your prayer life? In this section, I will share with you some things you need to know about moving to that new level in your prayer life. If you want to go further with God than you have ever been, then read and implement the truths discovered in these chapters. They have taken me to new heights in my prayer life, and I know they will do the same for you.

What Does It Mean to Call upon the Lord?

Remember: Prayer shows that you are depending upon God. Prayerlessness demonstrates that you depend upon yourself. Are you a praying Christian or a prayerless Christian? Are you depending upon yourself, or are you depending upon the Lord? Calling upon the Lord in prayer indicates that you are a praying Christian who depends upon the Lord.

Too many evangelical Christians would view this concept of calling upon the Lord as a foreign practice. What does it mean to call upon the Lord? The word *call* in the Old Testament means "to summon His aid." When you call upon the Lord, you are summoning, or inviting, God's aid to come into your life. This word *call* also means to cry out loudly in order to get someone's attention. This indicates that God wants you to call out loudly to Him like you really need His help. Pride will not permit you to call upon the Lord, but humility opens the door for you to move to a new level in your prayer life. When you call upon the Lord, you are inviting His activity into your life.

The word *call* also means "to shout." This principle calls for us to shout to God in prayer. You may view shouting as a disruptive and irreverent practice, but remember, I am talking about shouting to God in prayer. You shout at a pep rally. You shout at a ball game. The Bible teaches that one day God is going to call us home to heaven "with a shout." Please understand what I am sharing with you here. I am sharing what the Bible says when it uses the word *call.*

There is another word in the Old Testament Hebrew language for *call* that refers to calling upon the Lord in a public worship setting on the Sabbath Day. I interpret this to mean that the day of worship that we celebrate should be a day when we call upon the Lord by summoning His aid into our lives. In the church that you attend weekly, how many minutes in the service are allotted for Christians to call upon the Lord?

This is one of the great things I learned from the ministers of the Brooklyn Tabernacle Church. They give opportunities for their people to come before the Lord—summoning Him, inviting Him to be involved in their lives. This practice may be unique to us, but it is not foreign to the Word of God.

I believe that one of the sad commentaries on Christians today is that many only desire "neck-up" religion. They want their intellect increased and disregard emotion as needless. Your goal should be balance in regard to intellect and the heart. Refrain from labeling fellow believers who may be out of balance one way or another. They are not the issue. God's Word calls upon each Christian to call upon the Lord.

I want you to notice how the word *call* is used in several scriptural passages. Jeremiah 29:11–13 says, "'For I know the plans that I have for you,' declares the LORD, 'plans for welfare and not for calamity to give you a future and a hope. Then you will *call* upon Me and come and pray to Me, and I will listen to you. And you will seek Me and find Me, when you search for Me with all your heart'" (emphasis mine).

God's Word affirms that He has a future and a hope for everyone who calls upon Him. Our goal should not be to seek this future or this hope but to seek God in prayer by summoning His aid into our lives with all of our heart.

The word *call* is used again in Jeremiah 33:3, which says, "*Call* to Me, and I will answer you, and I will tell you great and mighty things, which you do not know" (emphasis mine). When you are willing to call out loudly to the Lord, summoning His aid into your life, God will do great and mighty things.

When you are willing to call out loudly to the Lord, summoning His aid into your life, God will do great and mighty things.

Psalm 145:18 says, "The LORD is near to all who *call* upon Him, To all who *call* upon Him in truth" (emphasis mine). God does not play games. He wants His people to summon His assistance with truthfulness. In prayer, let God see your heart and hear your heart as you invite Him into your life for assistance.

The practice of calling upon the Lord began in Genesis 4:25–26: "Adam had relations with his wife again; and she gave birth to a son, and named him Seth, for, she said, 'God has appointed me another offspring in place of Abel; for Cain killed him.' And to Seth, to him also a son was born; and he called his name Enosh. Then men began to *call* upon the name of the LORD" (emphasis mine). The Bible is very clear that the origin of calling upon the Lord in prayer began in Genesis. Under the leadership of Enosh, people began to summon God and invite Him into their lives.

Another passage that I believe you need to consider today is Psalm 80:18, which says, "We shall not turn back from Thee; revive us, and we will *call* upon Thy name" (emphasis mine). In this verse, God's people declared that they were not going to turn back from God any-more. They cried out to God to give them new life so that they would call upon Him again in prayer. What Christianity needs today is revival in calling upon the name of the Lord. Perhaps pride and timidity are not the reasons Christians fail to call upon the Lord. The real reason is that they need spiritual revival.

Remember, prayer is work. The hardest thing you will ever do in your life is call upon the Lord in prayer. Satan's strategy is to get you involved in anything that will keep you from praying. Satan will make you sleepy, make your mind wander, make you find reasons you cannot pray, and make things come your way that will keep you from praying.

Determine today to begin to summon God's assistance into your life daily. Commit to being a genuine prayer warrior who will call upon the Lord in prayer. If you will follow this practice daily, you will move to another level in your prayer life.

When Should You Call upon the Lord?

Scripture is very clear that each Christian should practice calling upon the Lord in prayer individually and corporately. When should believers call upon the Lord? I want to highlight five situations in which Christians should call upon the Lord.

Call upon the Lord All the Time

Do you call upon the Lord all the time or only when you need something? Do you call upon the Lord out of conviction or out of crisis? Your spiritual life should not have to be in an intensive care unit for you to call upon the Lord. You should call upon the Lord all the time.

Is your life organized enough to spend time calling upon the Lord daily? Do you have a prayer plan that allows time for you to call upon the Lord in prayer? If you don't already have such a plan, the last chapter of this book will help you design a plan for prayer in which you can call upon the Lord each day.

In our church, we have begun to dedicate certain Sunday evenings solely to prayer. These evenings have been filled with God's power. My prayer of preparation for these evenings of prayer is always, "Lord, give me the spirit and burden for prayer." In these evenings, our church calls out to the Lord in prayer. As Christians, we need to be willing to speak out to the Lord in prayer in a public setting, to call upon the Lord earnestly and deeply.

Without any question, each Christian and each church should call upon the Lord all of the time. Calling upon the Lord continually demonstrates that we are depending upon the Lord rather than ourselves.

Call upon the Lord in a Time of Need

Just as parents love for their children to call upon them in a time of need, God loves for His children to call upon Him in a time of need. Calling upon the Lord in a time of need does not indicate a lack of faith but an understanding that God is the ultimate object of our faith. God can do anything, anywhere, and at any time. He can provide for your need.

What kind of need do you have today? I do not believe God categorizes our needs as big or small. At times, we may be tempted to handle the small things and let God handle just the big things. It is as if we are saying, "God, we know You are really so busy that we will bother You with just the things that we know we cannot handle by ourselves." This attitude is wrong. God wants us to come to Him at all times to pray about all of our needs.

What is your need today? Do you need healing? All healing takes place because of God. Do you need money? Honor Him with what you have, and He will provide for your need. Do you have a relationship that is strained? Only God can bring two hostile or opposing persons together. The cross shattered all walls between persons. Do you have a material need? Call upon the Lord! He is able to meet even your material needs. Bear your heart to Him in prayer by summoning His aid into your life. Remember, God can make a way when there seems to be no way.

> Bear your heart to Him in prayer by
> summoning His aid into your life.
> Remember, God can make a way when
> there seems to be no way.

I believe that God creates needs in your life for the purpose of causing you to depend upon Him. He wants you to rely upon Him. He wants to do the impossible. He loves to show others that with Him all things are possible. Even before your need exists, God already has the supply. Call upon the Lord in a time of need.

Call upon the Lord in a Time of Pursuing the Future

Some of the most important decisions you will make in your life have to do with planning your future. If you are still young, in the future you will have to make decisions pertaining to college, career, marriage, and children. If you are middle-aged, you will have to make decisions pertaining to the care of your parents and your children, job opportunities or career moves, and even retirement. If you are in the senior years of your life, you may have to make decisions regarding where you live, what kind of care you want, and how close you want to be geographically to family members. Regardless of your age, the future demands that you make decisions.

My son Josh had a phenomenal high-school football career. As a high-school quarterback, he set statewide and national records for passing. Although many smaller schools would have loved to recruit Josh, he had his heart set on a career in major college football. Our family was before the Lord for almost a year about God opening up opportunities for Josh.

Josh's five-foot-eleven stature became a barrier in those final weeks of recruiting. More than forty major universities had contacted Josh, but one by one they backed away from him due to his smaller stature.

Josh called upon the Lord. Nick called upon the Lord for his brother. Jeana and I called upon the Lord for Josh's future. It was truly a family affair of prayer.

As I am writing the final pages of this manuscript, I am able to rejoice that God has answered our prayers. Josh is going to play major college football. However, God is going to pave a different path for Josh to follow so that He alone will receive greater glory when Josh succeeds on the next level.

When pursuing your future, call upon the Lord. He is able to give to you guidance and wisdom in regard to your future. The Bible promises you a great life, wonderful welfare, and God's peace as you call upon the Lord in prayer (see Jer. 29:11).

One of the pivotal questions each person must ask pertaining to his or her future is, "God, what do You want me to do?" My life is not my own; I belong to God. I am not owned by any man or any system. I am not the property of this world. I am God's property. Since He owns the title to my life, I must take directions pertaining to my future from Him.

The only way that your future is secure is when you call upon the Lord. He will come when you invite Him to be a part of your life. He will help you walk through all of the transitions of your life. He will provide you peace when you feel there is no way that peace can exist. He will be there for you in your future when no one else will. Therefore, trust Him. Rely upon Him. Call unto Him. Summon Him. Invite Him to make your future and all of its decisions very clear to you.

Call upon the Lord in a Time of Worship

In moments of public worship, are you calling upon the Lord? Is your day for worship set aside for the purpose of calling upon the Lord? When you go to worship at your church, call upon the Lord. Summon Him to meet with you and the entire body of Christ that is sharing that experience with you. The day of worship should be set aside as a day in your life that you call upon the Lord in prayer.

Much of the worship in church life today is stale and powerless. As a result, lives are left unchanged. Could this be happening because we do not spend time calling upon the Lord in worship? Much of worship today centers on personalities and performance, rather than the Lord and His work in the lives of people. Prayerlessness indicates dependence upon ourselves. Worship should never be about ourselves. Worship should exalt the Lord Jesus and be focused on calling upon Him in prayer. Call upon the Lord in a time of worship.

Call upon the Lord in a Designated Prayer Time

Do you have a designated time of prayer in your life? As I mentioned previously, make a date with God daily. Find a plan to follow, such as the one outlined in the last chapter of this book, that will instruct you on how to pray.

First things first! Get alone with God at the first of the day. Use this time to call upon the Lord in prayer. Let it be the time every day when you bare your heart to God about your life and your greatest needs in life. Take the time to listen to what He says to you as you bare your heart to Him.

> First things first! Get alone with God at the first of the day. Use this time to call upon the Lord in prayer. Let it be the time every day when you bare your heart to God about your life and your greatest needs in life.

Appeal to the pastors and leaders in your church to set aside services that are dedicated solely to prayer. God can do more in a moment of prayer than in all the programs one church could do in a lifetime. Determine to make your church a praying church. Decide today how you can walk alongside your pastor, helping him create a fellowship of believers who practice calling upon the Lord in prayer. I can assure you that his office is not being flooded with calls by people who want to help him make the church a praying church. Stand up and be different. Be a Christian who calls upon the Lord in prayer.

Prevailing Prince of Prayer

During my visit to the Brooklyn Tabernacle Church, Jim Cymbala mentored me in prayer. I watched him with his people. I watched him in worship. We talked a lot about prayer. I learned a great deal from him about prayer.

In between one of the services, Pastor Cymbala handed me a booklet entitled *Daniel Nash: Prevailing Prince of Prayer*. This booklet, written by J. Paul Reno, would be very worthy of your time to read. It will stir your heart to pray and to change.

Who is Daniel Nash? Perhaps you will be able to answer this question more accurately. Have you ever heard of a great evangelist by the name of Charles Finney? If not, let me tell you briefly about both of these men.

Charles Finney was a converted lawyer. Finney's life was so changed by the power of Christ that he never counted on anything other than prayer to win lost souls to Christ. According to this booklet, 80 percent of Finney's converts stood the test of time and were committed to Jesus Christ all the way to the end.

In later years, Dwight L. Moody was converted to Christianity. He was a shoe salesman who became a great evangelist and pastor. Fifty percent of Moody's converts stood the test of time.

Evangelist Billy Graham stated recently that if 20 percent of his converts stood the test of time in their commitment to Jesus Christ, he would be pleased because of the spiritual depravity of our culture.

When I read this information, I immediately asked myself one question: "Why did 80 percent of all of Finney's converts stay committed to Jesus Christ?" I discovered the answer. Charles Finney had a prayer warrior who traveled with him everywhere he went. Many times, this prayer warrior would go into the city or region two to three weeks ahead of the evangelistic emphasis that Finney would lead. He would rent a room and gather two or three saints of God from that city to prostrate themselves before God in prayer for their city or region. They would call upon the Lord in prayer, agreeing for God to do a mighty work of revival and evangelism in their midst. The power of God was evident before Charles Finney ever came to town.

Daniel Nash was this prayer warrior. You do not read about him in history like you read about Charles Finney, Dwight L. Moody, or one day you will read about Billy Graham. In fact, you may never read about Daniel Nash at all. Let's get it straight: Although the percentage of Finney's converts is a subject of debate, no one disputes that Daniel Nash was the key to Charles Finney's evangelistic accomplishments. He became known to some as Father Nash. Others referred to him as "The Prevailing Prince of Prayer."

Daniel Nash expended his life calling upon the Lord in prayer. History records that many times people would hear him as far as three-quarters of a mile away calling unto the Lord in prayer for the souls of many people in that city to come to Jesus Christ. Inscribed on Daniel Nash's tombstone are the following words: *Laborer with Finney. Mighty in Prayer.*

What an awesome statement to have written about your life! Daniel Nash was a man of prayer who understood the value of calling unto the Lord.[2]

Are you ready to move to another level of your prayer life as we move into the twenty-first century? I certainly hope so. It is time for all believers to learn the value of calling upon the Lord.

Who is going to be the Daniel Nash of the twenty-first century? How many people of this present generation will take on the burden and ministry of Daniel Nash? Most people expend their lives on things that really do not matter at all. Will you give your life, your all, to being a Christian who has a passion to call upon the Lord in prayer?

Chapter 8

How to Pray
It Through

In the early nineties, I sensed that God wanted me to communicate through writing the message that He was developing in my life. The hand of God was upon the ministry in Springdale, Arkansas. Other venues for ministry were opening across America and even some across the world. The television ministry expanded into more than sixty million homes across America. Opportunities were abounding.

Being a published author was not an ego trip for me. I wasn't primarily concerned with being known as a published author; instead, my insatiable passion was to get the message of God to everyone, and I felt that publishing was taking advantage of one of the great means of communication in our day. I wanted to share the message of God that He had been developing within me for years.

Little did I know at the time, but there were countless thousands of people who had this same passion. As those of us who have been published know by experience, the ego is attacked greatly through the process of publishing. You can think you have done a great work, but many times publishers just do not agree. You can think you have written it just right, and they will notify you that it would be better if you did it another way.

Upon the release of my first book, *Reconnecting,* I participated in the summer convention of the Christian Booksellers Association. By the time I left that place, I was really humbled. I realized that it would take a miracle of God for my book to reach a wide audience. There were thousands of new releases available that summer, and my book was just one among the many. I came home discouraged, just knowing that my days were numbered in Christian publishing.

What you hold in your hand is the fifth published trade book that God has permitted me to write and have published. What I once thought in that large convention center has not been the reality. By God's grace, He has allowed me to share the message that He is still developing in my life. I am very grateful.

It was through Christian publishing that God taught me the contents of this chapter. Back in the late eighties, I began the journey of wanting to write a book. I became so desperate that I published a book myself. That is a long story of acting ahead of God.

As my zealous and selfish desires of the late eighties became my zealous but selfless desires of the early nineties, I learned something great. I learned that I just needed to pray it through. I did not need to kick a door down, but I needed to pray persistently. Since what was once driven by ego was no longer driven by ego, I felt that the only hope I had was to pray it through.

Through the process of persistent praying, God began to open doors for my books to be published. My burning passion to get God's message out is real, so I spend time praying things through. Even the publishing of this book happened because I learned the value of praying it through.

What does it mean to pray it through? By the time you conclude reading this chapter, I believe you will understand what this means. As you consider how to pray something through, you may be wondering . . .

How Long Should You Pray for Something?

I do not believe there is a Christian anywhere in the world today that has not asked at one time or another, "How long should I pray for something?" Years ago, a movement was running rampant across the Christian arena that taught that if you really had enough faith you would only have to ask God for something once. Asking Him more than once indicated that you were full of doubt; therefore, God would probably not answer your prayer. I believe this teaching is in total contradiction to the teaching of Jesus Christ.

Why do Christians struggle with the question of how long to pray for something? I believe Christians struggle with this question for three reasons. The first reason is . . .

The Issue of Faith

Every growing Christian wants to live by faith. However, when a prayer request has been continually presented to God with no apparent response, a tension also pulls deep within us. This tension has to do with the subject of faith. How long is too long to pray about something? Does my need to keep praying indicate a lack of faith? Where does faith fit into what I am presenting to the Lord in prayer?

There is another reason we struggle with this question of how long to pray for something. The second reason is . . .

The Issue of Guilt

If you are any kind of prayer warrior, you know that you will continually battle with Satan in your life. In fact, you will do some of the toughest battles with him while you pray. Many times he will come to you while you are praying and attempt to discourage you. He will tell you, "If you had any faith, you would not keep on asking God about that." Or Satan may say, "Your heart is filled with doubt, so God is not going to answer your prayer."

*If you are any kind of prayer warrior,
you know that you will continually battle
with Satan in your life. In fact, you
will do some of the toughest battles
with him while you pray.*

All of a sudden you begin to wonder, *How long should I pray for this?* Guilt begins to flood your soul because you are asking God about it so much of the time when you talk to Him.

There is another reason why Christians ask God this question . . .

The Issue of Uncertainty

When you do not know how long you are to pray for something, you experience an element of uncertainty. When you operate in the lane of uncertainty, your faith seems to come to a standstill. Uncertainty breeds doubt in your life.

The issues of faith, guilt, and uncertainty do not need to invade your heart. So how long should you pray for something? You need to pray it through!

What Jesus Taught about Praying It Through

Jesus was the Master Teacher of prayer. Your prayers and your prayer life should be a mirror of His prayers and His prayer life.

In the Scriptures, Jesus taught us the following truth about prayer:

> He said to them, "Suppose one of you shall have a friend, and shall go to him at midnight, and say to him, 'Friend, lend me three loaves; for a friend of mine has come to me from a journey, and I have nothing to set before him'; and from inside he shall answer and say, 'Do not bother me; the door has already been

shut and my children and I are in bed; I cannot get up and give you anything.' I tell you, even though he will not get up and give him anything because he is his friend, yet because of his persistence he will get up and give him as much as he needs. And I say to you, ask, and it shall be given to you; seek, and you shall find; knock, and it shall be opened to you. For everyone who asks, receives; and he who seeks, finds; and to him who knocks, it shall be opened. Now suppose one of you fathers is asked by his son for a fish; he will not give him a snake instead of a fish, will he? Or if he is asked for an egg, he will not give him a scorpion, will he? If you then, being evil, know how to give good gifts to your children, how much more shall your heavenly Father give the Holy Spirit to those who ask Him?" (Luke 11:5–13)

When you understand this parable, you will know what it means to pray it through. Let me place this passage in context for you.

One of Jesus' disciples admired His prayer life so much that he asked Him, "Lord, would You teach us how to pray?" Jesus immediately responded by teaching the disciples what is called the Lord's Prayer. After He presented this model prayer, Jesus used a masterful illustration.

Suppose you had a friend who came to your home unexpectedly at midnight. This friend did not have anything to eat the entire day. Since you were unaware of his visit, you were not prepared to give him anything to eat. Desperate to find some food to offer him, you cross the street to a neighbor's house and began to knock on your neighbor's door. You yelled to your friend, "I need three loaves of bread." Your neighbor was sleeping when you awakened him and yelled back at you, "Leave me alone! My family and I are trying to sleep, and I am not going to get up and give you anything." You were tempted to walk away from the house, but you decided not to do so. Instead, you knocked on the door again and repeated your request. Because of your persistence, your neighbor eventually got out of bed and gave you whatever you needed.[1]

After giving this illustration, the Master Teacher, Jesus Christ, makes the following declaration: "And I say to you, ask, and it shall be given to you; seek, and you shall find; knock, and it shall be opened to you" (v. 9).

The literal translation of this in Greek, the original language of the New Testament, reads something like the following: "Ask *and keep on asking,* and it shall be given to you. Seek *and keep on seeking,* and you will find. Knock *and keep on knocking,* and the door will be opened to you."

> He wants us to be persistent in our prayers—to keep on asking, to keep on seeking, and to keep on knocking until God answers our request.

I want you to pay close attention to what Jesus is saying to us about prayer. He wants us to be persistent in our prayers—to keep on asking, to keep on seeking, and to keep on knocking until God answers our request.

Asking is a very important element in prayer. When you ask God for something in prayer, you are recognizing His authority over you and submitting your request to Him in faith that He will answer. Seeking is another important element in prayer. Jesus taught you not only to ask Him for things in prayer but to seek after God in prayer. If you need a job, it's not good enough to pray, "Lord, I need a job. Give me a job. You know my phone number, so have them call me." This is a low view of God, because He wants you not only to seek Him in prayer about the job but to pursue it at the same time. Knocking is another important element in prayer. Knocking indicates that you go beyond asking and seeking in going after what you need. Jesus taught you to ask and keep on asking. He taught you to seek and keep on seeking. He taught you to knock and keep on knocking. Jesus was teaching the importance of not giving up in prayer—the importance of praying something through.

Think back to Jesus' masterful parable of persistence. When you ask someone for bread, you are submitting to their authority to give you the bread. When you are seeking, you are traveling to the neighbor's house for the purpose of having your need for bread met. When you are knocking persistently at your neighbor's door, the neighbor will meet your need.[2]

As the Lord Jesus instructed His disciples in prayer, He began to ask them some questions. He asked, "How many of you as fathers would give your son a snake if he asks you for a fish?" (see v. 11). My children know I am no snake handler, so they would definitely not receive a snake. Then Jesus asked, "If your children ask you for an egg, how many of you would give them a scorpion?" (see v. 12). I do not handle scorpions either, especially after I was bitten by a brown recluse spider recently. As a father, I do not know another father who would ever give these kinds of gifts to his children. Then Jesus turned the discussion into another question in relationship to the heavenly Father: "If you, since you are evil, know how to give good gifts to your children, *how much more* shall I as your heavenly Father know how to give good gifts to you?" (see v. 13).

Jesus assures us that the heavenly Father will be a better father to us than any earthly father could ever be to his children. God always knows what is best for you. Just as you would only give to your children what they need, your Father in heaven will only give you what you need. God is the perfect Father.

What does all of this teach you about prayer? I believe the truth of this passage will be discovered when you . . .

Identify the Principle

What does it mean to pray it through? How long should you pray for something? In his excellent book entitled *When God Doesn't Answer,*

Woodrow Kroll goes to the heart of the matter: "If persistence was the key to the unwilling heart [of a neighbor], how much more effective will persistence be to the willing heart of God?"[3]

Do you remember when the man first asked his neighbor about the bread, and his neighbor responded, "Get out of here, it is midnight!" Yet he pursued his need being met. It seemed as if the neighbor almost got up but chose not to do so. But the man just knocked and kept on knocking on the door. Was the neighbor's heart willing to assist him? It appeared not! However, Jesus taught that if the key to the unwilling heart of your neighbor is persistence, how much more effective will persistence be to the willing heart of your heavenly Father? If the unwilling neighbor is finally going to give you what you need due to your persistence, then how much more would your Father meet your needs when you pursue Him persistently?

What does it mean to pray it through? How long should you pray for something? The answer is in this principle.

The Principle of Persistence in Prayer

The entire passage of Luke 11:5–13 has one basic teaching: If you ask and keep on asking, seek and keep on seeking, and knock and keep on knocking, God is going to hear your prayer and meet your need. God will honor your persistence in prayer as He comes alongside of you to help you be successful in your life.

In this passage, *persistence* means to be steadfast, to continue, to persevere, to endure, or to be tenacious in prayer. Jesus was saying to His disciples and to us, "Do not give up in prayer." Pray it through! Jesus wants you to persevere in prayer. Even when you do not want to go on, just go on praying. Jesus wants you to endure in prayer. When you want to quit, just keep on praying. Jesus wants you to be tenacious in your prayer life. Hold on to the promise in the Bible and do not let go until God absolutely closes the door and tells you emphatically, "No!"

Jesus was saying to His disciples and to us,
"Do not give up in prayer." Pray it through!

How do you pray something through? You pray with great persistence. Just like I told you in the opening paragraphs of this chapter, praying it through is what got every one of my books published. God is attracted to a believer who never gives up in prayer.

In the remaining paragraphs of this chapter, I want to attempt to answer the all-important question I mentioned earlier.

How Long Should You Pray It Through?

This is the major question that must be answered in concluding this chapter. I want to suggest to you that you pray something through until one of the following three things occurs. Pray it through . . .

Until You Know It Is Not God's Will

Since God speaks to you through His Word and your circumstances, you should pray it through until God affirms to you that it is just not His will for your life. If the Word is not for it, do not bother to even pray about it. You must remember: God's Spirit will never lead you opposite of God's Word.

Some years ago, I was asked to consider taking a position away from the pastorate in the evangelical world. This position was a position of great influence and vision. As soon as I was approached about this position, I felt God wanted me to draw aside in fasting and prayer in order to pray it through. The position was highly visible, so I did not want even to be considered if I knew God did not want me to do it. I prayed it through until I knew for certain that it was not God's will for my life. I called the person who wanted me to talk with this search committee and with confidence informed him that I really sensed it was not God's will for my life, so I would not let my name be considered for the position.

For those seven days, I was persistent before God in prayer. By praying it through, God affirmed me as a pastor and confirmed that the position was not His will for me. I was committed to go on with God in prayer until I prayed it through. God does not always answer that quickly, but I am thankful that He did.

I want to encourage you to pray your burden through until you know it is not God's will for your life. Pursue your dream. Activate your passion. Get before God and stay there until you know it is just not right in the eyes of God. If it is God's will, you will soon know. If you do not know, do not do it. When in doubt, don't! This is an important rule to follow in your life. Pray it through until you know it is not God's will.

You should also pray it through . . .

Until God Answers Your Prayer

Pray it through until you know the doors are shut tightly. Pray it through until you know it is just not right. Pray it through until God says no or until God says yes. Sometimes it is difficult to let it go when you know God says no. Yet when He says no, walk away. The worst place you can be spiritually is somewhere God does not want you to be in your life. Pray it through until God says yes. Thank God for the times in life when your persistence in prayer resulted in God saying yes. What an encouragement! What faith is created through God saying yes to our persistent praying.

If you are praying for someone who does not know Christ, then claim God's expressed desire in 2 Peter 3:9: "The Lord . . . is patient toward you, not wishing for any to perish but for all to come to repentance."

God is willing for all persons to repent of their sin and be saved. He does not want anyone to perish. Therefore, upon the authority of

God's Word, you know it is God's will for this lost person to be saved. So pray it through! Claim this verse before God. Hang on to it! Remind God of what He said. Pray with confidence, believing that God will save this person.

Elaine had prayed for Jim for more than forty years to come to Jesus Christ. She prayed with great passion and persistence for her lover and husband. Through the years she was tempted to get discouraged, but she clung to the promise of 2 Peter 3:9. Finally, in a unique way, God prepared Jim's heart. In God's way and in His timing, God prepared him to be saved. Jim came to Jesus Christ after forty years of his wife's persistent prayers for him. Elaine prayed it through until God answered her prayer about Jim. She practiced the principle of persistence in prayer. This is just what Jesus taught her in Luke 11.

Whatever you are facing today, pray it through until God gives you the answer. Do not stop! Hang in there and pray. Pray with persistence. Pray with faith! You may be praying for your house to sell, but it has not sold. Keep praying until God gives you the answer. You may be praying for a new job. Keep praying until God gives you the answer. You may be praying for a financial breakthrough. Keep praying until God gives you the answer. You may be praying for someone's salvation. Keep praying until God comes through. Yes, pray it through! Pray with persistency.

How long should you pray something through? Pray it through . . .

Until God Releases You

Many times what you pray about is a burden to you. I believe a burden is something that you go to bed with, wake up with, and live with all through the day. (No, I am not talking about your spouse!) I am talking about something that is very heavy on your heart. I have learned recently that you should pray that burden through until God releases you. If He does not release you from that burden, then keep on praying persistently about it.

When Nehemiah learned of the condition of Jerusalem, he was burdened for his homeland's main city. This was truly a burden as he entered days of fasting and prayer. He continued with that burden until God released him. God did not release him until he completed the task of rebuilding the wall around Jerusalem. This all occurred because he prayed it through. He kept on praying about it until God released him.

The burden that God gives you is a wake-up call. If God gives you the burden, it signifies He is active in the situation. Therefore, you keep praying it through until He releases you. How do you know when He releases you? He releases you when the situation is answered just the way you have prayed for it. He releases you when the situation is irreparable. He releases you when He removes your burden and replaces it with His peace. You will know when He releases you. Until then, pray persistently!

Do not give up in prayer. Keep on praying until God releases you. Sometimes that burden may last one year, ten days, or even forty years. Yet pray until God releases you. Persistent prayer is effective prayer.

> Do not give up in prayer. Keep on praying until God releases you. Persistent prayer is effective prayer.

Persistency in your prayer life demonstrates that you have great faith in God. It does not indicate a lack of faith. Persistency in prayer develops your character. It does not show you are inferior or prone to worry. Persistency in prayer guarantees God's activity—not in the sense that He will answer it the way you want it answered or even that He will answer it at all—but by indicating that God is active in the situation as long as He wants you to pray it through. Stay involved in prayer until God speaks to you in the situation.

Do you want to move to a new level in your prayer life? I hope so. One of the great ways that you can move to a new level in your prayer life is to learn to pray things through. Remember, you have a perfect Father in heaven who is willing to meet your needs. So pray them through! Give God the opportunity to receive the glory when you can announce to others that He answered your prayer as you prayed it through. I promise you, this will help you take a quantum leap in your prayer life.

Chapter 9   ■

HOW TO PRAY
FOR ONE ANOTHER

From the moment I first met Helen Graham, I knew that she was a very special woman. Godliness was her apparel. Her gray hair was truly her crown of glory. Everyone who knew Helen loved and respected her.

Helen Graham was a very special person for many reasons. When I followed God's call to the First Baptist Church of Springdale, Arkansas, she was a member of that church. She loved young people, so that is where she spent her time on Sunday mornings during the Bible study hour. She loved worship, so the choir was her place in the Sunday worship services. If Helen was healthy, she was present and praying.

I was only thirty years of age when I accepted God's call to this rather large congregation. I followed a very godly and gifted leader who had invested sixteen years of his life in leading this church into spiritual greatness. The transition was challenging, but the church made the transition in a wonderful way because of people like Helen Graham.

Helen Graham loved the pastor of her church, regardless of who the pastor was. She had a respect for the office of the pastor like few people do today. The reason for this was that she was a great woman of prayer.

Every time I saw Helen, she encouraged me and assured me of her prayers for me. She devoted the senior years of her life, not to criticism but to intercessory prayer. Helen always wanted to know how she could pray for me. Intercessory prayer was not a "put-on" for her; it was the passion of her life. Because of Helen's faithfulness, the glory of God was all over her life.

In 1996, I addressed the Southern Baptist Convention in the New Orleans Superdome. I was assigned the pivotal message, the convention sermon. I took this assignment very seriously. I did not want simply to prepare an impressive sermon that my peers would applaud, but I wanted to have a true word from God that would shake the convention.

I really sensed that God wanted me to fast and pray for forty days so that I would be prepared to receive His message for this convention. In this fast, I truly sensed that I was standing in the gap between God and the largest evangelical denomination in the world. The burden was great upon me to relay His message to this denomination, which consists of more than forty thousand churches composed of more than sixteen million members. This convention, which is attended mainly by pastors, staff members, and lay leaders, was an outstanding opportunity for any preacher.

God really impacted my life through my forty-day fast. I sensed His message for these convention messengers. As I preached the convention sermon on that Wednesday morning, God fell upon the Superdome with His favor. I can honestly tell you that it had nothing to do with me but everything to do with our sovereign God, who was attentive to the prayers of His people. I sensed God's leadership to offer an altar call at the conclusion of my sermon, which was a call to action for Christians and churches to get serious about meeting God through prayer and fasting for the purpose of spiritual renewal for our churches and our nation.

The response was God-sized! Lives were impacted. Some churches were truly changed, as evidenced by the testimonies that have been shared with me. God did more than I ever asked Him to do. It was truly a "God moment."

Why did this happen? Prior to that event, several members of my church committed to fast and pray for that specific moment. While I was in New Orleans, our worship center became a mighty place of prayer for the time of the convention sermon. Many of our laypeople gathered to agree in prayer and to intercede for me and the preaching moment before the Southern Baptist Convention. I thank God for the people who dedicated that day to the ministry of intercessory prayer.

On that strategic morning, Helen Graham committed to be part of this time of intercession. Toward the end of the prayer meeting, Helen prayed. When she returned to her place in the worship center, she had a stroke, and God soon called her home.

> If you want to move to another level in your prayer life, then you must learn how to pray for one another.

This is truly an amazing story. Helen Graham gave the senior years of her life to intercession. In fact, she spent one of the last moments of her life praying for God to fall upon the convention in New Orleans. She expended her life for the cause of Christ and for intercession for God's people.

Helen Graham knew how to pray for others. She was not content merely to pray for herself; she wanted to move to the high level of praying for others. If you want to move to another level in your prayer life, then you must learn how to pray for one another.

What Is Intercessory Prayer?

The term "intercessory prayer" may not mean a great deal to you, but it is vital to your Christian life. I believe one of the highest callings in the Christian life is the call to intercession—to pray for others. This call comes to every Christian who is growing in their faith.

When you intercede for others, you plead or offer petition on behalf of another person who is in trouble or in difficulty. You get before God in a very serious mode of prayer. When you are before God in this manner, you are praying for others who may really need your prayers.

Therefore, intercession is when you offer a prayer on behalf of another person or a group of persons. An intercessory prayer asks God to meet with them and to provide for their need. Intercessory prayer is not focused on yourself but on others. It is a call from God to stand in the gap between a holy God and a person in need. Intercessory prayer is one of the highest callings in the Christian life.

Due to the "me-driven" cultural Christianity that is rampant in churches in the world today, Christians do not hear a great deal about intercessory prayer. In fact, in most churches the term and the practice have been placed on the shelf. What we want is to have others pray for us, meet our needs, teach us, help us, fill us, and have God touch us. The focus is always on ourselves and our interests. This self-centered Christianity is a far cry from what God teaches in His Word.

What Is an Intercessor?

An intercessor is a Christian who prays for another person. When the Holy Spirit places a person upon your heart to pray for and you are obedient to pray for that person, you become an intercessor. When you pray for your church, you become an intercessor. Every growing Christian will perform the ministry of intercessory prayer. As you grow in your faith, the Holy Spirit will place certain people upon your heart so that you will pray for them.

Are you an intercessor? Do you let the Holy Spirit place persons upon your heart so that you can pray for them? If you are a parent, you should intercede for your children. If you are a grandparent, you should intercede for your children and grandchildren. If you are married, you should intercede for your spouse. As a Christian, you should intercede for your local church and for the work of Christ around the world. You should also intercede for your country. Undoubtedly, each growing Christian will become an intercessor by faithfully praying for others.

Two Insights

When you pray for others, you move into a high moment in the Christian life. Each Christian who intercedes in prayer does so in many ways. I believe that two insights must be understood by anyone who wants to be an effective intercessor. The first insight is that an intercessor must . . .

Pray Specifically

Are you a parent? If so, have any of your children ever come up to you and asked, "Mom and Dad, will you just meet my needs today?" Probably not, because then you would have to spend time trying to guess what they want you to do. Children usually articulate specific needs to their parents. There is no need for a guessing game. They are requesting you to meet a specific need.

When you pray for others, you need to pray for their needs specifically. This means that you will need to know those needs in order to pray for those needs specifically. Effective intercessory prayer articulates specific needs of others. You are not to pray, "Lord, help this person. Bless him." This kind of generalized praying is neither productive nor effective.

> When you pray for others, you need to pray
> for their needs specifically. Effective interces-
> sory prayer articulates specific needs of others.

For several years, I have participated in a ministry in our church called "Warriors on the Wall." This prayer ministry involves members who are committed to pray one hour a week for the ministries of our church as informed and instructed through a monthly mailing. Personal accountability is built into the ministry because someone calls each week to remind fellow intercessors of their time on the wall. Once I have completed my weekly time of intercession, I call another person to continue to the prayer wall.

For several years, I have called a man in our church each Sunday morning at 6:00 A.M. As I commend him to the wall of prayer for our church, he always asks me, "How can I pray for you specifically this week?" Billy Ussery understands this insight of praying specifically. He wants to pray for my needs specifically when he prays for me.

The second important insight about intercessory prayer is . . .

Pray Biblically

One of the most effective ways to pray for others is to pray specific biblical passages for people. Pray according to God's will for their lives. You can know God's will in prayer by studying the Scriptures. Pray biblically for others by praying according to God's revealed will in the Scriptures.

Pray the Word of God into the lives of other people. Ask God to give you a verse that He may want you to pray for them. You can always ask the person you are praying for to give you a Bible verse to pray into their life.

Pray for people straight from the Word of God. Pray the Bible into the lives of other people. How can you pray the Word of God into their lives? Let me show you how this can be accomplished.

How to Pray for One Another

You can learn a great deal about prayer by evaluating the prayers of other people. When the apostle Paul described his prayers for the church in Colossae, he gave us an example of how to intercede for others. Colossians 1:9–12 records Paul's prayer:

> For this reason also, since the day we heard of it, we have not ceased to pray for you and to ask that you may be filled with the knowledge of His will in all spiritual wisdom and understanding, so that you may walk in a manner worthy of the Lord, to please Him in all respects, bearing fruit in every good work and increasing in the knowledge of God; strengthened with all power, according to His glorious might, for the attaining of all steadfastness and patience; joyously giving thanks to the Father, who has qualified us to share in the inheritance of the saints in light.

This prayer illustrates three specific and biblical ways that you can pray for others. The first thing that you can pray for others is for them to . . .

Be Filled with God's Will

Paul prayed that these Christians would be "filled with the knowledge of [God's] will" (v. 9). Why was this so important?

There was a very detrimental philosophy in Paul's day known as gnosticism. This anti-Christ philosophy taught that man could attain a higher knowledge of God and that salvation came by this special knowledge. Paul's prayer for the Colossians was not to have superior knowledge, but for them to have "God knowledge," a full knowledge that is discovered in the will of God.

The problem at Colossae was a lot like the problem in many modern churches in America. At times, spirituality in the American church is equated with some kind of superior knowledge about the Bible. Knowledge in and of itself is not the source of spiritual power and understanding. This is why it is important to pray that others are filled with "God knowledge," the knowledge of His will.

The Holy Spirit imparts the wisdom of God. Paul prayed for these Christians to be filled with the knowledge of God's will "in all spiritual wisdom and understanding" (v. 9). Spiritual wisdom is applying God's knowledge to life's situations and seeing life from God's perspective. Spiritual wisdom is dependent upon the knowledge of God's will. For spiritual wisdom to be realized in your life, you must know what God says in His Word and how His truth applies to situations in your life.

Spiritual wisdom is applying God's
knowledge to life's situations and seeing
life from God's perspective.

Spiritual wisdom should be accompanied by understanding. To have spiritual wisdom with understanding is to use this information to make wise decisions in your life. Good decisions are made from "God knowledge," not human knowledge. This is why quick decisions can be detrimental to your life.

Take the time to discover the facts and information about what is going on. Know what God says about it in His will. Do not seek to have mere human knowledge but "God knowledge." Pursue the will of God and His wisdom in your life.

When you have the privilege to intercede for other people, pray for them to be filled with the knowledge of God's will. Pray for them to have "God knowledge." Pray for them to discover God's will in His Word. Pray for them to see life the way God sees it. Pray for them to have spiritual wisdom and understanding. Pray for them to be able to gather the needed information for their situation and then proceed to discover the will of God.

Whether you are praying for your spouse, your children, your friends, your church, or your country, it is fitting to pray that these people are filled with God's will. Another thing you can pray for others is for them to . . .

Walk in God's Ways

As you pray for others, pray for them to walk in God's ways. The way a person walks is the way that they witness. If they do not walk in the right manner, they cannot witness with integrity. In his prayer for these fellow believers, Paul prayed for them to walk in a certain way. How should you pray for people to walk in God's ways? Pray for people to walk . . .

Worthily

Paul prayed that the Colossians would "walk in a manner worthy of the Lord" (v. 10). The only way to walk worthily in the Lord is to walk in the ways of the gospel message with the goal of pleasing the Lord. Our intercessory prayers should not be, "Lord, help this person to do what they want to do" or, "Lord, help this person to be satisfied in life." These prayers do not honor God. The intercessory prayer that should be prayed is, "Lord, help this person to walk in a manner worthy of You and to please You in all respects."

Your goal is not to be the public relations person for your church. Your goal should be to please the Lord in all things and to live a life worthy of Him. Your goal is to please God, not men.

As you pray for others, pray for them to walk in God's ways in a worthy manner. Pray for them to represent the gospel in every way in their life. Pray for them to please the Lord at all times. Another way that you can pray for them to walk in God's ways is for them to walk . . .

Fruitfully

Paul prayed that the believers in Colossae would be "bearing fruit in every good work" (v. 10). For you to bear fruit means that you will bear fruit of the seed. The seed is the Word of God, which was placed in you at salvation. This seed is also the person of the Holy Spirit, who is the down payment given to you at salvation and guarantees your future inheritance.

You are to bear fruit of this seed of salvation by living a holy life. You are to bear fruit of the seed by reproducing the life of Christ in you into the lives of others. You are to bear fruit by winning others to faith in Jesus Christ. God does not want you just to be faithful; He wants you to be fruitful. A faithful Christian is a fruitful Christian.

When you pray for others to walk in God's ways, ask God to help them walk in a fruitful way. Another way that you can pray for them to walk in God's ways is for them to walk . . .

In Maturity

Paul prayed that the Colossians would be "increasing in the knowledge of God" (v. 10). The only way you can get to know God is to increase in your understanding of God that is revealed in His Word. Through the practice of prayer—talking to God and listening to what He says to you—you can get to know God more intimately. This is the process of maturing in the Lord.

Are you maturing in the Lord? Are you further along with God than you were one month ago? A year ago? Real knowledge is not knowing more facts about God. Real knowledge is "God knowledge." It is demonstrating in your own life what God says in His Word.

When you pray for other people to walk in God's ways, pray for them to walk in a mature manner. Pray for them to walk in such a way that they will practice the Word of God and be ever-increasing in the faith.

One of the men who serves beside me is Bert Miller. Bert is a former businessman who in his latter years of life has chosen to serve the Lord's church in a full-time manner. He makes many decisions that have major impact upon our ministry. If I practice the principles of intercessory prayer that I have already laid out in this chapter, then I would pray for him in the following manner:

> Lord, I thank You and bless You for Bert. I pray for him to be strengthened today and filled with Your will in his life. I pray that he would be committed to hear what You say to him, not just what man says. I pray that his greatest passion will be to learn about You by being nurtured in You. May You continue to draw him to Your Word so that when he makes decisions for his life, his family, and our church that he will be filled with the knowledge of Your will. I pray that he will be able to take Your Word and apply it to his life. God, fill Bert with Your will. May his wife see a man who walks in Your ways. May his children and grandchildren see a man who walks in Your ways. I pray for him to walk worthily, fruitfully, and in maturity. Help him to desire to learn Your knowledge through Your power. In the name of Your Son, Jesus Christ, I place these requests before You for my friend Bert. Amen.

As you intercede for others in this manner, you will rejoice as you see God mature this person and progress him in his faith. This is the power and result of intercessory prayer. The Lord instructs you to pray that others would be filled with God's will, walk in God's ways, and . . .

Be Strengthened with God's Power

Paul prayed that the believers in Colossae would be "strengthened with all power, according to His glorious might" (v. 11). When you pray for others, pray for them to be strengthened with God's power. Pray for them to experience the power of God in their lives. As you pray for others in this way, you are praying for them to be strengthened in God's power so they can be . . .

Steadfast

Paul prayed that the Colossians would attain "steadfastness" (v. 11). When you pray for others to be steadfast, you are praying for them to be faithful. This means that God will endow them with His power to bear up under affliction. Whatever they are going through in life, God will give them the power necessary to see them through. God wanted them to be strengthened with His power so they would be steadfast and also so they could be . . .

Patient

In addition to steadfastness, Paul prayed that the Colossians would attain "patience" (v. 11). Patience can only take place in a person's life when he or she is being strengthened with God's power. When the person you are praying for is suffering or facing an injustice in his or her life, this person needs to be able to put off his or her fury. This is what it means to be patient. It means to be able to put off your fury through the challenges of life. When you are praying for a person to be patient, you are praying for that person to be nonretaliatory, regardless of what others do to him or her.

> When you pray for others, pray for them to be strengthened with God's power. Pray for them to experience the power of God in their lives.

Pray for others to be patient. This kind of patience cannot exist without the power of God. God's power is the only way that one can become patient. God has instructed you to pray for others to be strengthened with God's power so they can be steadfast, patient, and . . .

Thankful

Paul prayed that these Christians would be "joyously giving thanks to the Father" (vv. 11–12). God's power enables you to be thankful in life. As a Christian, thanksgiving should flood your heart because Christ's sacrifice on the cross has qualified you to live forever with God.

One of the missing ingredients in this present generation is thankfulness. The entitlement mind-set plagues our churches, our families, and our government. When people think they are entitled to certain things, they will not be thankful. God's power gets Christians beyond this deceit and trains them to be thankful.

When you have the privilege of interceding for others, pray for them to be strengthened with God's power so that they will be steadfast, patient, and thankful.

Just a few pages ago you read an example of prayer for my friend Bert. Permit me to illustrate this again by interceding in the following way:

> Lord, help my friend Bert to live a life that shows that You are strong. May he know that You are not attracted to strength but to weakness. Take this frail and weak man and strengthen him with Your power. Grant him faithfulness and patience. Help him not to retaliate but instead to permeate the character of Christ. Remind him periodically of how he was once a sinner but now he is a saint of God. May his heart be thankful when he remembers what You have done for him. Amen.

When you pray for others, pray for them specifically and biblically. Pray for them to be filled with God's will, to walk in God's ways, and to be strengthened with God's power.

> Take up the call to be an intercessor. There is
> not a higher moment of prayer than when
> God leads you to pray for others.

Will you be open to God's Spirit calling to you to pray for other people? Will you hear Him speak to you about the importance of praying for others? Will you let Him speak to you about whom He wants you to pray for in your life? Will you learn to pray for others specifically and biblically?

Take up the call to be an intercessor. There is not a higher moment of prayer than when God leads you to pray for others.

Who Will Step Up?

I have often wondered about who is praying for me now like Helen Graham prayed for me. In God's sovereign way and by His will, I am certain He is raising up someone to pray for me as Helen used to pray for me.

Who will step up now? Who will step up and pray for me? Who will step up and pray for others? Who will step up and stand in the gap for other people?

Will you be the one? God told Ezekiel, as recorded in the twenty-second chapter of his book, that He searched all over the land for one man to stand in the gap for His people, but He could not find one who was willing to do so. I hope this tragic indictment cannot be said about you or me in respect to our families, our friends, our churches, and our country.

We need to be praying Christians. We need to be Christians who pray for others—the kind of Christians who experience the high calling of intercessory prayer. Prayer becomes much more of a ministry to you than for you, far beyond what you could ever imagine. Praying for others will move you to a new level in your prayer life!

Chapter 10

How to Do
Warfare Praying

When I was a young preacher, I had several opportunities to preach the Word of God in my region. People were so gracious to put up with me. I believe my enthusiasm is what drew them to ask me to preach because my content was probably rather questionable. All I did was rear back and preach what I knew to be true.

One of the opportunities that came my way was to preach at a vibrant African-American church that was hosting an area-wide youth rally. I had never attended this church, so I was in for a real treat. The singing was rather lengthy, and I was the last of several preachers. When my time came, I preached all I knew to preach. The more they praised the Lord, the longer I preached. It seemed like I preached and preached and preached some more. As long as they appeared to enjoy it, I just kept on preaching.

An older preacher preceded my time to preach. He was preaching against Satan that night and made a statement I have never forgotten. He said, "If you are not having a head-on collision with the devil every day of your life, that probably means you are going in his same direction."

What a word! I have never forgotten what that man said. I do not remember his name or even the name of the church, but I have never forgotten that statement. This statement is really true about the Christian life. If you are not having a head-on collision with the devil every day of your life, then you are probably going in his same direction. Satan is very strong. He comes against you in many ways. If you are not colliding with him regularly, then you had better check out where you are spiritually. The last place you want to be going is in his same direction.

The Principle of Spiritual Conflict

Most Christians assume that all conflict is bad. Yet, this is just not so. I have been a Christian for more than twenty-five years. The observation that I want to make is so true. Would you commit to memory the statement you are about to read? **The closer you get to God, the more spiritual attacks you will face in your life.**

This principle may seem strange to you, but it is reality! I thought for years that my problems would be solved if I would just pray more and be with God more in my life. I thought that conflict was bad and only happened when something was not right in my life. In fact, I faced a lot of guilt when conflict did occur.

The closer you get to God, the more spiritual attacks you will face in your life.

I saw this principle lived out in my early years of serving as a pastor. I was consumed with enthusiasm to reach the community with Christ. I guess my enthusiasm was somewhat contagious because usually the vast majority of the church wanted to assist in the task of taking the gospel to the community. I would lead the church to pray and lead the church to witness. Both of those spiritual disciplines were very important. I thought everyone would agree.

Little did I know, not every person in the church wanted to share the gospel with the community. Not every person in the church wanted to get before God in serious prayer to pray for the lost of the community. I do not know if my seminary classes did not teach me that not everyone would want to evangelize and pray, but if they did, I was asleep or not listening. Quite honestly, I was absolutely surprised that not everyone was fired up to make a difference for Jesus.

What occurred was spiritual conflict. Years ago, I equated this conflict with certain people, due to my own immaturity, but now I know better. This conflict came from Satan, the devil, our enemy. I did not understand as a young pastor what the problem was, so I would try to convince everyone in the church to come along with us. I would use all kinds of persuasive techniques in the pulpit, most of them even spiritual, but the conflict still occurred every time we tried to do something for God.

I kept wondering, *Why is this conflict occurring? Why don't these people want to embrace Jesus' mission for His church?* Then I began to learn the principle of spiritual conflict. I began to understand that the closer I got to Jesus, the more spiritual attacks I would face in my life. I began to understand this principle of spiritual conflict as it related to the church. The closer the church got to the Lord by doing His will, the more spiritual attacks the church would face. As serious business was taking place to win the lost to Jesus, I realized that Satan was not just going to hand people over to the Lord without a fight. When I began to understand this principle of spiritual conflict, I began to be freed from the guilt I had experienced. I also began to gauge the success of our ministry not so much by our numbers but by the level of disarray that Satan attempted to cause within the church.

In these last few weeks, I have tried to remember this principle as I have been writing this book. The spiritual conflict has been enormous.

The demons of hell are coming out of the closet to distract me from God's mission for me in writing this book. My name has shown up on the editorial page of several newspapers. Television interviews that I have granted have ended up in disarray and imbalance. Bizarre and crazy events have surrounded me. As I was speaking about these attacks with my wife, Jeana, she reminded me that I needed to remember that I was writing a book on prayer and the last thing the devil wants is for Christians to pray.

In this chapter, I will be covering exciting ground. Yet I need to remind you that the ground is sprinkled with land mines. However, you can make it through if you will just pray as you read this chapter and be ready for the impending attacks of the evil one.

This chapter is for Christians who really want to move on with God. It is for Christians who want to do some serious praying to God. It is for Christians who want to move to a new level of spiritual growth in their prayer life. Get ready! I am praying that God will teach you in this chapter how to do warfare praying. Before you read on, pause for a moment and pray a prayer to God something like this:

> Dear Lord, I want to learn how to do warfare praying. I want to learn how my praying can penetrate the territory of the devil. As I read the remaining pages of this chapter, cover me with the blood of Jesus Christ. Let nothing happen to distract me from completing this chapter and implementing its content. I surrender these moments to You. You are Lord. Yes, You are greater than our enemy Satan. In Jesus' name, teach me how to do warfare praying. Amen.

I have prayed a similar prayer in writing this chapter, so I really encourage you to pray a similar prayer in reading it. This chapter is not written to appeal to your intellect or curiosity about the subject of warfare praying; it is written to lead you into the journey of doing warfare praying.

This chapter is for Christians who really want
to move on with God. It is for Christians
who want to move to a new level of spiritual
growth in their prayer life. Get ready!

Warfare Praying Consists of Praying against Satan

One of the most familiar passages of Scripture concerning spiritual warfare is Ephesians 6. This chapter describes what is known as the spiritual armor of the believer. The verses that precede the description of the believer's spiritual armor are especially insightful: "Finally, be strong in the Lord, and in the strength of His might. Put on the full armor of God, that you may be able to stand firm against the schemes of the devil. For our struggle is not against flesh and blood, but against the rulers, against the powers, against the world forces of this darkness, against the spiritual forces of wickedness in the heavenly places" (vv. 10–12).

Since the Word of God serves as our authoritative source for faith and practice, let's investigate what the Bible says about praying against the power of Satan.

One thing you need to understand is how limited you are in relationship to Satan's power. He is much stronger than you and can overcome you. You are inadequate in and of yourself to overcome his power. He will defeat you if you attempt to whip him in your own power.

This is why Ephesians 6 calls for you to be strong in the Lord and in the strength of His might. This means that you are to have God's power in your life as you pray against Satan. You are to operate at a high spiritual level by being empowered by the Holy Spirit rather than by yourself. If you are in Christ, your authority is great. You have the name of Jesus as your banner, the blood of Jesus as your covering, and the Word of God as your sword. You are prepared to pray against Satan when you are being controlled by the Spirit.

When you lose the battle against the devil in your life, it is because you are operating in your own strength. Defeat comes as a result of your choice to handle your own affairs, rather than to let God handle them for you. Even though defeat may come periodically in your battles against Satan, it is always God's intention to grant you victory through His power flowing through your life.

One of the alarming things happening in the church is that believers are asleep and rather lethargic about being in a war with the devil. Status quo and defeat are accepted as the norm in the Christian life, rather than being seen as abnormal. If your spirit is down and your heart is experiencing some despair, understand that you are in a war! Satan is out to destroy your life. You are not to wave the white flag in surrender to him, but you are to stand firm against his schemes (see 1 Pet. 5:8–9). Each one of his schemes has the ultimate goal to bring you down in your life. As you are in a spiritual war, stand your ground against Satan. Do not surrender anything. In fact, be aggressive enough to take back what you may have already surrendered to him.

Satan is real. He is cunning and sly. He is the angel of light. He will not walk down the aisle of your church and say, "Look at me everyone—I am the devil." You often cannot recognize him because he is the greatest con artist ever to have existed. Remember, he exists to bring you down.

More can be understood about your enemy when you understand what his name means. The name *devil* means "accuser and slanderer." Satan does all he can to malign you, your name, and, most of all, the name of Christ and His church. He is the one who comes and whispers in your ears thoughts like, *You can't win. You can't do it. You can't live the Christian life.* He wants to make you question all you are doing in your life, especially those things that are right. He will bring people into your life who will operate his scheme, which is to bring you down in some way. These people may say or write things about you that are not true at all.

The people who come against you in this manner are deceived. They are tools in the hands of the devil and do not know it. These people can even have good intentions. They may even be people who are close to you—people you love. For example, it could be your father, who always has a way of putting you down. It could be your mother, who never encourages you and constantly tells you how you should have done things in another way. It could be your children, who are struggling with authority and periodically have their tongues ablaze with accusations about what a poor parent you are. It could be your boss, who has the gift of criticism and exercises it with you daily. Their goal seems to be to choke life out of you with their hateful words, rather than put life into you through encouraging words.

This is why it is so important that you are careful with your words. When you are accusing someone of something, be careful. Remember, Satan is an accuser. If you choose to slander someone's character, be careful to remember that Satan is a slanderer. Do not participate in maligning someone else. Satan is Mr. Maligner.

This is why the Bible instructs you to remember that your enemy is not flesh and blood, but Satan. "Flesh and blood" is a reference to people (v. 12). This may be difficult for you to grasp, but you never fight against people, but against Satan. If you can prick the finger of someone and it bleeds, this person is not your enemy. Your enemy is Satan.

This struggle that you will face with Satan calls you into hand-to-hand combat against him. This combat will not take place on earth but in the heavenly places, where you pray against the spiritual forces of darkness and wickedness. You have been raised up to live in the heavenly places in a spiritual sense. It is here, in the heavenlies, that you do this warfare praying.

One of the best ways to prepare for combat is to know everything you can know about your enemy. You need to study your enemy thoroughly, along with his tactics and strategies. You can never assume you know these things. If you do, defeat is inevitable.

What You Need to Know about Your Enemy

There are four critical facts about Satan that you need to know. These four facts are . . .

You Are in a Spiritual War with Satan

Let me reaffirm to you that you are not in a war with people. Stop seeing people as the source of your problems and conflicts. You are in a spiritual war with Satan. If you don't wake up and go into combat, you will be continually defeated.

Satan Is Your Only Enemy

You need to understand that Satan is your only enemy. It is critical that you stop viewing persons, institutions, systems, and circumstances as your enemies. Yes, Satan can operate through each one of these, but the essence of your problem lies with the spiritual force of darkness, Satan himself. Put on your spiritual glasses and begin to see what God sees. Satan is your only enemy.

Satan Wants to Destroy You, Your Family, Your Church, and the Work of Jesus Christ across the World

Satan is never interested in building you up. He does not desire for you to experience victory or success. He wants to destroy every person in this world so they will experience an eternity of destruction with him in hell.

He wants to destroy your marriage. Your spouse is not where the combat really is; your war is against Satan. Satan is ending as many marriages as he can. Satan will do anything to take out the man of God called your pastor. He hates men of God. This is why so many pastors are falling to the lure of gold, glory, and girls.

Satan wants to destroy the church. This is why so many churches are in never-ending battles over insignificant things. The church is to be a unified body of Christ, but this is rarely the case due to the level of division going on in the body of Christ.

Satan wants to do anything he can to put a stop to the work of Jesus Christ around the world. He does not want the Good News told, so he will get the church involved in many good things in order to keep them away from the main thing of taking the gospel to the world.

Satan wants to do anything he can to put a stop to the work of Jesus Christ around the world. Yes, Satan is out to destroy all he can. You are his target!

Yes, Satan is out to destroy all he can. You are his target! If you are questioning whether this is reality, you are right in the middle of his deceitful plan. Satan has deceived you, and you have bought his lies. Remember this about Satan: He always plays for keeps. His wins are not just short-term wins. Many times his wins are eternal.

Even Though Satan Is Alive and Well Today, His Doom Is Certain

Satan is tearing up and wrecking lives all across the world today. It is very obvious how destructive he is when you witness the dysfunctional relationships in every segment of society. Our enemy is wreaking havoc upon our culture. We read daily about the torment and adversity that he is bringing into the lives of people. He appears to have the upper hand in the lives of people everywhere. Yes, Satan is alive and well.

However, Satan's doom is certain! One day, the evil one will be thrown into hell once and for all. When Satan points you to your past, which may be filled with defeat and despair, you should point him to his future, which will be finalized with certain defeat. As a believer in Jesus Christ, you will win in eternity and Satan will lose.

This is why your praying can be warfare praying. Periodically, you need to pray something like the following:

> Lord, I stand against the power of Satan in my life today. I declare him powerless over me because I am a child of the King. I am born again by Your Spirit. I am forgiven because I am covered with Jesus' blood. So Satan, I stand against you in Jesus' name. You have no authority over me, my family, or my church. You are a defeated foe. You have no authority in my life. In Jesus' name, I stand my ground. Amen.

This warfare praying calls upon God for strength. It reminds Satan that you are not to be his prey because of what Jesus has done for you. This kind of praying equips you not to give up any ground at all to Satan in your life. This kind of praying will lead you to experience true spiritual victory.

As you perform warfare praying, it is important to be covered daily with the armor of God. As I mentioned in chapter 1, one of the spiritual practices I follow daily is to place God's armor upon the members of my family. Since I am up most days before the rest of them, I dress them spiritually for the day even before they get out of bed. As the spiritual leader of the home, I have the responsibility to put the armor of God upon my family. How do I do this? I pray in the following manner:

> Dear God, please gird Jeana, Josh, Nick, and me with Your truth today. Place on us Your righteousness, which is in Jesus Christ, not in me. Place on our feet the preparation of the gospel of peace today so that everywhere we go we are sharing Your love with someone. Place us behind the shield of faith at all times today so that we can escape the fiery missiles of Satan that will come against us. Wherever the missiles come from, may Your

shield protect us. Fill our hearts with Your Word, which is our only offensive weapon against the enemy. Use the prayers of others for us today to lead us to victory. Thank You, Lord, for covering us from head to toe and from back to front with Your spiritual armor. In Jesus' name, amen.

This kind of praying brings rest upon your heart, knowing that you have placed the members of your family under the armor of God. They are now truly dressed for spiritual success. They are ready to face the day and even the devil. The armor is now on, and they can stand firm against their enemy.

Warfare praying consists of praying against Satan. But there is more to warfare praying.

Warfare Praying Consists of Praying against Strongholds

What is a spiritual stronghold? A stronghold is an area of your life that you have given over to Satan. Would you take a moment to read that definition again? A stronghold could be a habit, a bad thought, or even a vain imagination in which you followed your own selfish desires and fulfilled the lusts of your flesh. These expressions are against the will of Christ and are expressions of disobedience to God's Word.

A stronghold could be a habit, a bad thought,
or even a vain imagination in which you
followed your own selfish desires and
fulfilled the lusts of your flesh.

When you give in to the desires of your flesh, you usually think that it is no big deal. However, the moment that you give in to your flesh, Satan gains some ground in your life. Eventually, this area of your life can imprison you. The results can be devastating to you spiritually.

This is why you deal with the same sins over and over again in your life. You confess them to God repeatedly, yet you have no victory. This creates a defeatist attitude spiritually where you eventually accept mediocrity in your faith. Satan convinces you that this is "just you" and that you cannot ever overcome these sins because they are just a part of your human nature. What has occurred is that Satan has built up a fortress in your life. Every time you disobey God in this area, Satan gains a little more ground in your life. This is a stronghold!

Would you imagine with me for a moment one of the speakers to your home entertainment system? When you look at that speaker, all you see is a wooden case covered with some kind of cloth. All you know is that sound comes out of that speaker when it is activated. This speaker has the power to penetrate your home with sound. If you were to remove the cloth, you would be able to see the speaker. Otherwise, all you see is the cloth.

This is what a stronghold is like. The real issue is the difference between what God sees and what you see. For example, you see the cloth over the speaker. Only when the cloth is removed do you see the speaker itself. With or without the cloth, the function of the speaker is the same. This is the same way it is with a stronghold. A stronghold is the difference between what God sees and what you see. What do I mean?

For example, what you see is worry about finances. What God sees is a stronghold. What you see is fear of the future. What God sees is a stronghold. What you see is bitterness because you have not been able to forgive someone. What God sees is a stronghold. What you see is pornography, whether it comes in the form of magazines, videos, or the Internet. What God sees is a stronghold.

When the Lord opens your spiritual eyes to see what He sees and removes the cloth, you will begin to recognize that many of these sins are major strongholds in your life. At some point in time you handed a specific area of your life over to sin, and Satan gained ground in your life. From God's perspective, you will see a stronghold in which Satan's wicked power resides in your life. Yes, he can influence your mind, your will, and your emotions.

The Bible is very clear about spiritual strongholds. Second Corinthians 10:3–5 describes this struggle: "For though we walk in the flesh, we do not war according to the flesh, for the weapons of our warfare are not of the flesh, but divinely powerful for the destruction of fortresses. We are destroying speculations and every lofty thing raised up against the knowledge of God, and we are taking every thought captive to the obedience of Christ." What does this passage mean in relationship to spiritual strongholds?

Would you take a moment and touch your arm with one of your hands? Would you touch one of your legs with your hands? This is your flesh. The Bible says in these verses that you cannot war against the spiritual strongholds in a physical way. If you try to fight the devil with your own might, you will lose. We are just not powerful enough on our own to overcome the power of Satan.

God has given you some weapons to use in this spiritual war. In a few moments, you will read about some of these spiritual weapons God has given to you. The problem is that when the world takes up fleshly weapons against you or your flesh, you are tempted to retaliate immediately with your flesh. Your weapons of warfare are divinely powered. Your flesh is not empowered like this. The Bible says that your spiritual weapons are so powerful that they can destroy spiritual fortresses or strongholds. This means that you can regain the ground you gave up by your sinful choices by using your God-empowered spiritual weapons to destroy strongholds.

The Bible says that these spiritual weapons can even destroy various speculations or imaginations that we have in life. An example of one of these vain imaginations would be when you think, *I wonder what they think of me?* In time, you begin to imagine things that may not even be true. Before you know it, a devastating paranoia begins to take place in several areas of your life. How many times have you imagined something to be a lot worse than it really turned out to be? You may justify this kind of thinking by saying, "Well, I am just playing it safe. I wanted to prepare myself for the worst possible scenario." The problem with speculations or vain imaginations is that you are not able to enjoy the present life because you are too busy worrying about what might happen in your future.

The Bible goes on to say that all disobedience will be punished. When you get to heaven, your obedience to God will be ultimately complete and your disobedience will be ultimately punished. The secret to overcoming a spiritual stronghold in your life is to take captive every thought you have and place each of them under the Lordship of Jesus Christ.

The secret to overcoming a spiritual stronghold in your life is to take captive every thought you have and place each of them under the Lordship of Jesus Christ.

Yes, the Scriptures verify that God has given you some weapons to carry on this spiritual battle. Remember, it is not a fleshly battle, so you cannot fight it with the flesh. It is a spiritual battle that must be fought with spiritual weapons. As you pray against Satan and spiritual strongholds, you will be successful only when you use spiritual weapons.

The Weapons of Your Warfare

What are the weapons of your warfare? I want to mention five weapons that God wants you to use in your daily spiritual battles.

The Name of Jesus Christ

The name of Jesus is the most powerful name under heaven. You are to stand firm against Satan in the name of Jesus Christ. You are to destroy spiritual strongholds in the name of Jesus Christ. At the name of Jesus, Satan will flee and spiritual strongholds will be obliterated, regardless of their apparent strength. Activate the power of God by using the weapon of the name of Jesus.

The Blood of Jesus Christ

When Jesus died on the cross, His blood became the atonement for your sin; in other words, His blood covered over your sins. His blood was so powerful that His unblemished sacrifice became the provision for the forgiveness of your sins. If you want to make Satan angry, just sing about the blood of Jesus Christ. Remind Satan that you are covered with Jesus' blood and that you stand in His grace alone. The blood of Jesus is a spiritual weapon that can destroy any stronghold because all of your sins were paid in full on the cross.

The Word of God

The Word of God is the only offensive weapon in the armor of God. It is also the most powerful weapon because the battle comes down to God's Word versus Satan's word. God's Word is always more powerful than Satan's word. This is why it is imperative that you read the Word, hear the Word, grow in the Word, study the Word, and memorize the Word. Any time Satan comes against you with false accusations, speak the Word of God and he will flee. The Word of God is the truth. Satan is a liar, and he hates the truth. The Word of God is a powerful weapon in your spiritual artillery.

The Word of Your Testimony

Satan hates to hear your testimony of how Jesus Christ changed your life. This is why you are sometimes hesitant to witness. Satan has convinced you that you cannot do it or that your testimony is ineffective. Satan does not want to hear you recite what Jesus did for you on the cross. He realizes that the moment you share your experience of the life-changing power of Jesus Christ, people will want what you have. Then they will embrace the cross, and Satan will have lost another soul to God. Your testimony is powerful—share it with others and remind Satan daily how Jesus has changed your life.

A Love for God Greater Than the Desire to Live

Do you love your life? Do you continually try to preserve your reputation? Do you insist on claiming your rights?

The Bible tells you not to love your life (see Rev. 12:11). In fact, even if you are facing death for your faith, do not try to preserve your life. A unique spiritual power is activated when you do not love your life, even when you face death. Satan is overcome by this kind of courage. This demonstration of allegiance to Christ and denial of yourself can obliterate spiritual strongholds.

Closing Words

In closing, I want to share a few words from the living God that will bring Satan down and destroy all spiritual strongholds. Think upon them. Meditate upon them. Repeat them over and over again. These are the words of life!

■

> Therefore also God highly exalted Him, and bestowed on Him the name which is above every name, that at the name of Jesus every knee should bow, of those who are in heaven, and on earth, and under the earth, and that every tongue should confess that Jesus Christ is Lord, to the glory of God the Father. (Phil. 2:9–11)

For the word of God is living and active and sharper than any two-edged sword, and piercing as far as the division of soul and spirit, of both joints and marrow, and able to judge the thoughts and intentions of the heart. (Heb. 4:12)

They overcame him because of the blood of the Lamb and because of the word of their testimony, and they did not love their life even to death. (Rev. 12:11)

■

Yes, these are words of life! Words of power! Words of victory!

Chapter 11

How to Empower
Your Prayers

One early February morning in 1995, I was in my study having my personal time with God. While I was reading through *The One Year Bible* and asking God to speak to me through His Word, I was alarmed at what I sensed God was saying to me.

I observed in the Book of Exodus how God called Moses to go up on the mountain to spend forty days with Him in fasting and prayer. The result of this extended time of fasting and prayer was that Moses received the Ten Commandments. When Moses returned from His time with God, he discovered the people of God abounding in idolatry. Moses' heart was broken, and the Bible records that he returned to the mountain to spend another extended time with God in fasting and prayer. Although I have read that passage many times, on this particular day I became frightened at what I sensed God was calling me to do in my life.

As I was praying over this passage, I sensed that God was calling me to draw aside to be with Him for forty days of prayer and fasting. I sensed that God wanted me to concentrate in prayer and fasting for spiritual revival in America, in my church, and in my life. I was really taken aback by what I sensed that God wanted me to do. In fact, I told no one and inwardly hoped that what I heard was not a call from the Spirit of God.

During the next couple of days, I really struggled with God about this calling. I had not heard of many people who had ever fasted and prayed for that length of time. I had participated in fasting and prayer for many years, but the longest fast I had ever observed was only three days. Three days of fasting was one thing, but forty days seemed like an eternity.

After a few days of prayer over this issue, I was convinced that this calling to fast forty days was from God. I began to study and think through this time with God. I knew the timing was important in relationship to my schedule. I had many questions, but I had no one to ask.

On a Sunday morning in early March, I walked into my office and discovered a book on fasting and prayer on my desk. A dear brother named Rick Sparks, a man in my church who operates a Christian radio station, had come across the book and just sensed that God wanted him to give it to me. I was leaving town that day to preach a revival for a few days. I began to read that book eagerly, wanting to learn everything I could on the subject. It was another confirmation that God was calling me to fast and pray.

I decided to tell my wife what I sensed God was calling me to do. When I told her that I believed God wanted me to fast and pray for forty days, she said, "If God is calling you, I will support you." Her support was another confirmation that God was calling me to go on a journey with Him.

Upon completion of our annual ski vacation over the spring break season, I began to make serious and final preparations for this forty-day journey with God. I really felt that I needed a plan to pray for this time. I wanted a list of specific things that God wanted me to pray about during this time of fasting. I asked the Lord to make this plan and this list very clear to me. Within a day, the Lord had given me the plan of what I would do during these forty days.

As I've mentioned, I sensed that God wanted me to pray and fast for spiritual revival to occur in America, in my church, and in my life. The Lord gave me specific items for prayer concerning each one of those areas. I would spend most of the normal periods set aside for eating in prayer. As well, I would strive to spend two hours of uninterrupted time with Him every morning solely for this calling to fast and pray. I would interpret all hunger pains as a call to prayer. I would attempt to draw aside several times a day just to be with God, so I needed to adjust my work schedule to accommodate this need. I would tell no one but my closest staff and my family, from whom I would need understanding and prayer. In addition to this, I would journal all activity that occurred between God and me during this forty days. I also sensed that God wanted me to conclude this journey with Him in a personal retreat so I could solidify what He was going to do in my life during this time. Finally, the dates were confirmed in my heart for the journey to begin.

Blastoff! The journey with God began for forty days. What happened? I wrote more than one hundred pages in my journal, documenting God's mighty activity in my life. I sensed oneness with Christ like I had never experienced. My spirit was very sensitive to the Spirit of God. I experienced the mighty anointing of God upon my life and ministry. I began to refer to these days as "Forty Days That Changed My Life."

Blastoff! The journey with God began for forty days. What happened? I sensed oneness with Christ like I had never experienced.

What God chose to do in those forty days was remarkable. As I concluded that time in personal retreat with Him, I did not want to let go. I had been on a journey with God that was unprecedented. At the same time, I was involved with the details of life that seemed so mundane during that time.

On that final day, I had to travel to Atlanta for a very important meeting. As I was sitting on that plane, reflecting upon my experience, I began to write my final thoughts. The closing hour of the fast was coming upon me.

I did not want to leave the journey, but I knew it was time. That night, in an Atlanta hotel restaurant, I concluded my time of fasting and prayer. Very early the next morning, the Spirit of God woke me up. My heart was filled with celebration and praise. God came upon me in that room like I had never experienced before in my life. His grace fell upon me in a way that I cannot describe. Time seemed suspended. I do not know how long God and I dialogued that morning, but the oneness and fellowship with Him were incredible.

In case you decide to reach your own conclusions about my experience that early morning, I want you to know that I did not speak in tongues or any kind of prayer language. It was several days before I could even articulate what happened to me in that room. The power of God fell upon me with a new and fresh anointing, and my life and ministry have never been the same. Truly, it was one of the defining moments in my spiritual life.

I want you to also understand that I do not think the power of what happened that early morning is merely that one experience. I really believe that God graced me because of my humble obedience to Him. He loves a surrendered, broken, and weak life. In those final days of fasting, that is exactly what I was. God had everything in my life. I was totally surrendered. I was broken like never before. My body was weak, twenty-four pounds lighter, but my spirit was standing tall in oneness with Christ.

In that closing retreat with God, I really sensed that God was releasing me to tell my church about what God had done in my life. I wrote the entire membership, encouraging them to be in our church on Sunday, June 4, 1995, because I believed that it would be one of the monumental days in our church's 125 years of existence. I told them that I was going to speak on forty days that changed my life.

On that Sunday morning, approximately ten days following the conclusion of my forty-day time of fasting and prayer, God showed up like never before in my ministry. Within moments of worship, I sensed the Holy Spirit usher Himself into that room like a tidal wave. The power was unbelievable! On that morning, I repented of my sins. I stood in complete transparency before my people. I appealed to them to get their lives right with God so that revival could come into our church.

On that morning, our service lasted two and one-half hours. No one moved or left early. Time meant nothing because the Spirit of God was present among us. People were on their faces before God even before the public invitation began. Worship was powerful before the message and after the invitation. Incredible brokenness came upon the congregation. On that day revival came to the First Baptist Church of Springdale, Arkansas.

I was in a place where I had never been as a pastor. Of course, that was not surprising because I was at a time in my life like I had never been. I asked the people to return that evening to see what God would choose to do among us as we sought Him.

Seventy percent of the Sunday morning crowd came back on Sunday evening. (I told you that God moved!) When we assembled for the evening service, the Holy Spirit was again present among God's people. We whetted their appetites with stories of revival. I recounted some things God had shown me during my forty-day journey with Him. That evening, I saw openness and transparency in the church like I had never seen before. Many of God's people stood up before the church to repent of their sins, ask for forgiveness, and experience deep brokenness before God. Others who had been delivered from that sin joined them at the altar and covered them with prayer.

Yes, it was a profound evening in all of our lives. After four hours of true revival coming upon God's people, the Lord led us to close out the evening in unprecedented celebration. It was now past 10:00 P.M. on Sunday, but the people still wanted to sit around and talk about what God had done among us that day.

On June 4, 1995, God came to the First Baptist Church of Springdale. On that day, the church got a new pastor without changing pastors. On that day, I got a new church without changing churches. When God comes, things are never the same again. Audio- and videotapes of that day have been listened to and shown literally all over the world about what God did that day in our church. You can still receive copies of that pivotal day in our church from our ministry resource center.[1] It was a day that God was exalted!

On June 4, 1995, God came to the First Baptist Church of Springdale. On that day, the church got a new pastor without changing pastors. On that day, I got a new church without changing churches.

As I told our people following that first forty-day fast: God can do more in a moment than we could ever do in a lifetime. I believe that! My life and my ministry are living proof of that spiritual reality. I am astounded at how God has chosen to use my obedience to Him. Complete surrender to God leads to boundless opportunities to experience His grace.

God will probably not call most people to fast and pray for forty days, but I guarantee you that He will call most people to experience specific days of prayer and fasting. This calling from God must come from Him. If it does not, you will regret it completely. If He calls you, then you will have the power to do whatever He is calling you to do.

I want you to understand though that I do not believe that prayer and fasting are hoops that you jump through to get God's attention. God is not your puppet. He will not be manipulated. In addition, fasting and prayer are not something that others can call you to do. They may ask you to pray about whether God wants you to join them in fasting and prayer, but God is always the One who gives the calling to fast and pray.

As a pastor, I have often asked my people to join me in specific days set aside for fasting and prayer for specific needs in our church, for major events in our church, or for the purpose of evangelizing our region. Each of these has been connected to some specific needs in the body of Christ. Yet in each situation I have asked our people to pray about whether God would want them to join us in a day of prayer and fasting for the need that was upon my heart. I would encourage any pastor or spiritual leader to practice this with your people.

I would encourage all Christians to join your pastor in these days if he is convinced that God is calling the body to fast and pray over a specific need. God honors people who will practice fasting and prayer. I believe that fasting and prayer are God's gateway to supernatural power.

What Is Fasting?

Fasting is abstinence from food with a spiritual goal in mind. It is abstaining from the most natural thing your body desires—food—in order to entreat the God of heaven to do something supernatural in your life. God's entrance into His supernatural power is fasting and prayer.

In a practical way, fasting can also be abstinence from other things in life. For example, just think what would happen in your life if you fasted from television for one week. Just think what would happen in your life if you fasted from the Internet for one week. Whatever is important to you, fast from it for a time, and you will see God do something really great in your life.

I believe fasting is powerful because you humble yourself before God. The Bible commands us to humble ourselves: "Humble yourselves, therefore, under the mighty hand of God, that He may exalt you at the proper time" (1 Pet. 5:6). According to this scripture, you are to take the initiative to humble yourself before God.

The word *humble* means "to lie low, to make yourself flat, or to put yourself under." It indicates more of an action that you take, rather than a position you hold. There is a continual correlation in the Scriptures between fasting and humbling yourself before God. This is why David said in Psalm 35:13, "I humbled my soul with fasting." If you study the Scriptures thoroughly, you will discover numerous commands to humble yourself before God. You are to take the initiative to humble yourself before God. I believe one of the most specific and direct ways to obey this command is to humble yourself through fasting and prayer.

When Ezra was leading the Jewish exiles back to Jerusalem, an amazing event occurred beside the Ahava Canal. Ezra halted the travelers in order to seek God's protection on their journey: "I proclaimed a fast . . . that we might humble ourselves before our God. . . . So we fasted and sought our God concerning this matter, and He listened to our entreaty" (Ezra 8:21, 23). Ezra and the people were in a moment of crisis, so he proclaimed a fast for the people. Why? So that the people of God would humble themselves before God. As they fasted and prayed about their need, God answered them. What a great spiritual truth! Just as Ezra saw God's hand when the people humbled themselves through fasting and prayer, I have seen God's hand respond in my life in the same way.

What Does the Bible Say about Fasting?

The practice of fasting occurs throughout the Scriptures. In addition to the stories I have already shared, I want to recount for you a few more accounts of fasting in Scripture.

In the Old Testament, the Jewish people would fast on the most important spiritual day of their year—the Day of Atonement. They understood that fasting prepared and assisted them in this spiritually significant day in their lives. As I have already stated, Ezra fasted and received God's protection and power for God's people. In 2 Chronicles 20:3, Jehoshaphat proclaimed a national fast to seek the Lord for direction and protection. As a response to their fasting, God delivered His people. When Nehemiah heard the condition of things in Jerusalem, his great burden moved him to fast (see Neh. 1:4). In that time of fasting and prayer, God called him back to Jerusalem to rebuild the wall around the city. One of the greatest revivals in human history occurred in Nineveah as a result of fasting and prayer (see Jon. 3:5).

In the New Testament, John the Baptist fasted and prayed. The apostle Paul also practiced fasting and prayer. The early church as recorded in Acts practiced seasons of fasting and prayer. In Matthew 6:17, Jesus taught, "When you fast . . ." He did not say *if* you fast or *if you want* to fast, but He said *when* you fast. Jesus placed fasting on the same level as praying and giving. When Jesus was returning from the Mount of Transfiguration with Peter, James, and John, they noticed that the disciples were trying to cast a demon out of someone. They could not understand why they could not exorcise this demon. Jesus said that their unbelief was the obstacle that was keeping them from removing this demon from this person. But Jesus encouraged them and said that nothing is impossible with God (see Matt. 17:20). He shared with them that if they wanted the faith to do these kinds of miracles they would only receive this kind of faith through fasting and prayer. Yes, even through Jesus' own recorded forty-day fast He overcame the devil and his temptations and was empowered by the Holy Spirit.

The Bible is full of illustrations of fasting and prayer. If this spiritual discipline was good enough for Jesus, it should be good enough for you. If Jesus saw the need to humble Himself before the Father, certainly you should sense the same need.

The Bible is full of illustrations of fasting
and prayer. If this spiritual discipline
was good enough for Jesus, it should be
good enough for you.

I believe that one of the reasons that fasting is so disregarded and ignored by Christians today is because of Satan. Satan knows the power of fasting. He has attempted to keep this truth from the church and does so quite effectively. He has also tried to keep the attention away from fasting by creating senseless concerns about it.

For example, should a person talk about their times of fasting? No, not while they are fasting (see Matt. 6:16–18). However, Jesus does not forbid talking about the fast once it is over, if He directs you to do so in a God-glorifying way. Just think, if Moses had not talked about what God had said to him in his forty-day fast, you would not have the Ten Commandments. Enough said?

The Power of Fasting

In much of this chapter, I have written about the power of fasting. Fasting really does have the power to change your life. I believe it can even change your church. Yes, I believe it can even change our country.

Fasting is powerful because you neglect the flesh and its natural desire of eating in order to appeal to God to do something supernatural in your life. God always pours out His Spirit upon you when you neglect the carnal in order to pursue God. Remember, you are to pursue God—not revival, not fasting, not His supernatural power. God is the source of those blessings, but those blessings should never be more important to you than God Himself.

I believe that fasting is so powerful that it can set a person free who has been enslaved in some kind of sin and bondage. Fasting breaks any bondage a person has in their life. Personally, I have become convinced that the bondage that is occurring in the lives of many people will never be broken through countless sessions of counseling or hours of support-group assistance. I am not discounting the value of counseling and support-group ministry, but the problem is that a great amount of bondage exists as a result of demonic activity, especially in the areas of spiritual strongholds.

In my days of extended fasting and prayer, God has set me free from sins that had plagued me for years. Extended times of fasting make you aware of the holiness of God and the exceeding sinfulness of yourself. God has used fasting to break the chain of sin in my life, and I know He will do the same in your life. Why? Fasting empowers your prayers with real God power!

When Should You Fast and Pray?

I believe there are some specific times when God wants you to fast and pray. Do you have a desire to have a new and fresh touch from God? Do you have a desire to see God blow a fresh breeze of His Spirit upon your church? Would you like to see God bring a mighty spiritual revival to your country? If you would answer yes to any one of these questions, then it is time for you to fast and pray.

I also believe another time you should fast and pray is when you are desperate for God to do something supernatural in your life, your church, and your nation. Answer this question honestly: How desperate are you for God to do something supernatural in these areas? Along the way of life, God will create moments of desperation. The changes of life have a way of creating desperation. Illness, disaster, and tragedy have a way of creating desperation. These are desperate times in which we live. You need to be desperate for God to move in you and through you in these days. Desperation accompanied by fasting is hazardous to the devil's health and will transform your spiritual life.

Helpful Hints When You Fast and Pray

I want to share four helpful hints that you need to adhere to when you fast and pray. The first thing you should do when God calls you to a season of fasting and prayer is . . .

Discover God's Plan

Before you fast and pray, attempt to discover God's plan for you. He has a specific reason that He wants you to fast and pray. Attempt to define those reasons, regardless of the length of the fast. Remember: Fasting is abstinence with a spiritual goal in mind. What are the specific goals for your time of fasting? Write down those things that you sense God wants you to pray for during that time of fasting.

For example, if your fast is for one day, define three or four spiritual goals that you are praying for during this one-day fast. Write them on a card. Place them in your pocket or in your Bible. Look at it through the day. Let it become your prayer list. Have a plan whenever you pray and fast. If your fast is extended in length, then pray over your plan to pray every day, even several times a day.

Determine the Length of Your Fast

Attempt to determine the length of the fast before you begin. There has only been one time in all of my fasting that I did not know the length of the fast before I began it. I believe the magnitude of your need should determine the length of your fast. Read that statement again. Digest it. Let it become your guide for determining the length for your times of fasting.

Withdraw

Fasting without withdrawing to some degree will only provide limited results. I am not talking about leaving your life for a number of days. But you should withdraw more than normal to be with God during your fast.

If your daily time with God is normally thirty minutes in length, then make it sixty minutes the day you fast. Turn the times set aside for meals into prayer times with God. Withdraw with the Word of God in your hand, and talk to God without ceasing.

Journal

Whenever you fast, write down your thoughts in a journal. Every time you meet with God, journal what God has said to you in His Word. There is a certain release that comes when you journal what God is saying to you. This record of your spiritual life will become a real treasure for you. God will use it to create greater faith in your life as you reflect upon your journal and remember God's activity in your life.

You Only Have Four Problems

I believe every Christian only has four problems in life. You might say, "Only four?" Yes, I believe you only have four problems in your life.

I believe when God comes to live in you His Spirit resides in your spirit. In your spirit you are in complete oneness with Jesus Christ. When you fast, your spirit becomes very aware of the Spirit of God, who is united in oneness with your spirit. Your spirit also becomes sensitive to the needs around you. It also will stand up with a humble power unlike any other time in your spiritual life. So what are the four problems that interfere with this oneness with the Spirit of God?

When you fast, your spirit becomes very aware of the Spirit of God, who is united in oneness with your spirit.

The four problems you have in the Christian life are your mind, your will, your emotions, and your body. Your mind races away at times and thinks upon things that are not holy. Your will stands up periodically in opposition to God's will. Your emotions are like a roller coaster at times, measuring the ups and downs of your life. Your body is deteriorating every day.

Have you ever witnessed the orchestra conductor exercise his influence upon the orchestra? It is amazing! Whenever he lifts his arms in preparation to lead the music, the musicians raise their instruments in a single motion. Although the various members of the orchestra were each playing different notes and rhythms during the warmup, when the conductor lifts his arms they are immediately prepared to follow his direction.

When you fast, your spirit becomes like that orchestra conductor. Your spirit is connected in supernatural oneness with God and calls to attention your mind, your will, your emotions, and your body. Through this experience, your mind becomes the mind of Christ. Your will is aligned with God's will. Your emotions reflect the emotions of Jesus—whatever He loves you love and whatever He feels you feel. Your body, weak through fasting, is made strong through God's supernatural intervention.

Any one or all of those four problems can be restrained during times of fasting and prayer. You do not have a single problem that God cannot solve.

Fasting will definitely take your prayer life to a new level with God! Practice it and you will become a testimony of God's amazing supernatural power. Fasting will empower your life and your prayers with real God power![2]

Section
Four

BARRIERS TO
PRAYER

Chapter 12

THE WALL OF STRAINED RELATIONSHIPS

Jews and Gentiles have been at odds with one another for years. A wall existed between the two groups for centuries with little hope of its ever coming down. That wall was so deep that you could not tunnel underneath it, so tall that you could not climb over it. It was so thick that you could not break through it. This wall indicated a definite and serious separation between the two groups.

In the Book of Ephesians, the apostle Paul describes this wall that separates the Jews from the Gentiles. In this discussion, Paul reveals that this wall was finally broken down by the work of Jesus Christ on the cross: "But now in Christ Jesus you who formerly were far off have been brought near by the blood of Christ. For He Himself is our peace, who made both groups into one, and broke down the barrier of the dividing wall" (2:13–14). This wall was brought down by the power of Jesus Christ on the cross. He died to make all people one.

In this section, I will share about barriers that have been raised up to separate you from God when you pray. The goal you should have in your prayer life is for your prayers to be so effective that God hears them and answers them. In this section, I will share with you about . . .

What Must Come Down Before Your Prayers Go Up

The walls that are created by the sinful choices of people must come down before their prayers go up to God. The great news is that the work of Christ on the cross has abolished all the walls. Therefore, the walls can come down and your prayers can go up to God.

Dr. Oscar Thompson was a very influential man in my life. He was my evangelism professor at Southwestern Baptist Theological Seminary. He is now with the Lord, as he died with cancer in my last year of seminary work.

Dr. Thompson taught about the value of human relationships. He used to say that the most important word in the English language is the word *relationship*. In his wonderful book *Concentric Circles of Concern*, Dr. Thompson writes about the importance of developing relationships with people for the purpose of winning them to faith in Christ. As well, he taught about the value of relationships between believers in Christ. Dr. Thompson believed that love travels on the track of a relationship. Just as a train can run off the tracks if the tracks are not right, love will not operate effectively if the relationship is not right.[1]

One of the best examples of a pure relationship is the relationship of the Godhead: God the Father, God the Son, and God the Holy Spirit. The common belief among conservative, evangelical Christians is that there is one God who is in three persons. Incredible harmony exists between the persons of the Godhead. There is no division. There is no strain or even a hint of disharmony. There is no part of God who wishes He were another part of God. The Godhead is an example of true unity and peace. This is the kind of relationship that should exist between people.

God's will for all relationships is harmony. He desires for all people to love one another. God wants unity to exist between all persons. His death on the cross obliterated the walls that have existed between all persons. This is why God can bring unity and harmony in all relationships.

Prayer nurtures your relationship with God. Do you believe that your relationships with other people affect your prayer relationship with God? I believe the answer to that question is that there is . . .

A Spiritual Law That You Cannot Break

There are many reasons why some of your prayers are not answered. I believe one of the main reasons is because of strained relationships. The spiritual law that you cannot break in your life as a Christian is, God will not answer your prayers if your relationships with other people are strained. You cannot break this spiritual law if you expect your prayers to be answered. In this chapter, you will begin to see the reality of this spiritual law take place.

> The spiritual law that you cannot break in your life as a Christian is, God will not answer your prayers if your relationships with other people are strained.

With this spiritual law fresh on your mind, take time to evaluate your relationships with other people. How is your relationship with each member of your family? What about your relationship with your relatives? Your relationship with your coworkers? Your relationship with your neighbors? Your relationship with the Christians who attend your local church? Your relationship with the leaders of your local church? Are these relationships strained or unified?

Each Christian has the responsibility to be in a right relationship with other people. In Romans 12:18, Paul instructs, "If possible, so far as it depends on you, be at peace with all men." The burden is placed upon you. The blame game is unacceptable. Regardless of fault or problem, God places the burden on you to be at peace with all people.

If you violate this spiritual law, your prayers will not be answered. Satan builds up this imaginary wall in relationships, making you think that there is no way you can relate properly to certain persons. When this occurs, a wall is created between you and God that hinders your prayers from being answered. God will not answer your prayers if your relationship is strained with other people.

Evaluate your relationships with other people more thoroughly. Begin this evaluation process by looking at your . . .

General Relationships

When Jesus preached what is known as His Sermon on the Mount, He dealt extensively with the subject of relationships. He gave powerful instruction about how we are to relate to others. In Matthew 5:21–24, Jesus shares:

> You have heard that the ancients were told, "You shall not commit murder" and "Whoever commits murder shall be liable to the court." But I say to you that everyone who is angry with his brother shall be guilty before the court; and whoever shall say to his brother, "Raca," shall be guilty before the supreme court; and whoever shall say, "You fool," shall be guilty enough to go into the fiery hell. If therefore you are presenting your offering at the altar, and there remember that your brother has something against you, leave your offering there before the altar, and go your way; first be reconciled to your brother, and then come and present your offering.

These words from Jesus are penetrating words. Convicting words. Powerful words.

Jesus taught that murder was a sin and a violation of the court. Most of us would agree with that statement. But Jesus took it one step further and said that anger is as serious an offense as murder. In relationships, anger must be dealt with or the relationship will be strained at best or terminated at worst. The word *anger* in this passage refers to the kind of anger that is a settled condition of your mind without any intention of taking revenge. We tend to think of anger as an emotion that always explodes in outbursts. But this word for anger refers to the type of ongoing, suppressed anger that churns within you toward another person.

How does this anger ever come to the surface of your life? Jesus said it will surface in remarks such as, "That person is good for nothing" or, "That person is empty-headed." In these verses, Jesus said that if you are presenting your offering at the altar and remember that your brother has something against you, then you should be reconciled to your brother before you present your offering to God. If you have negative feelings in your heart toward someone else, then you cannot do serious business with God. Jesus instructed us to go and be reconciled to the people with whom we might have a strained relationship before we do our business with God.

If you want to do business with God in prayer, you must ensure as far as you can that the relationships in your life are right. There is no ground for you to get around the spiritual law concerning relationships. If you have something against a person, go and make it right with them immediately. If you know someone has something against you, go to them now and attempt to make the relationship right with them. Drive to their house. Make a phone call. Write a card. Send an e-mail. Do whatever it takes to get right with that person.

Communing with God is very serious business. It is holy business. Sin will not be tolerated in any form, even strained relationships. Here's a bold statement that you need to remember: **Do not bother to pray until you are right with others.**

Do not think you can compromise or negotiate this spiritual truth. God wants your heart pure when you talk to Him. He wants things right between you and others before you attempt to carry on business with Him. Are you wanting to do business with God? If so, consider this checklist right now: Do you have anyone in your family today with whom you have a strained relationship? Do you have a friend with whom you had perfect harmony, but now your relationship is strained? Do you have a strained relationship with someone in your church or your past church? Do not bother praying to God until your relationship with others is right. Strained relationships must be healed before your prayers can go up to God with the greatest effectiveness.

The most challenging place to live the Christian life is before your family. Let's enter into the privacy of your life today by looking at . . .

Family Relationships

One of the most spiritually convicting times for me is when I deal seriously with God about my relationship with my family. I believe this is true for all of us. I have been strongly committed to my family for years. Most of the people in my church would give a strong testimony about my sincere and diligent commitment to family life. Even with that strong commitment, I still get under the Holy Spirit's conviction about my relationship with my family members. I hope you do as well.

I want to highlight a very difficult passage of Scripture that concerns the importance of family relationships:

> In the same way, you wives, be submissive to your husbands so that even if any of them are disobedient to the word, they may be won without a word by the behavior of their wives, as they observe your chaste and respectful behavior. And let not your

adornment be merely external—braiding the hair, and wearing gold jewelry, or putting on dresses; but let it be the hidden person of the heart, with the imperishable quality of a gentle and quiet spirit, which is precious in the sight of God. For in this way in former times the holy women also, who hoped in God, used to adorn themselves, being submissive to their own husbands. Thus Sarah obeyed Abraham, calling him lord, and you have become her children if you do what is right without being frightened by any fear. You husbands likewise, live with your wives in an understanding way, as with a weaker vessel, since she is a woman; and grant her honor as a fellow heir of the grace of life, so that your prayers may not be hindered. (1 Pet. 3:1–7)

These words are stirring and relevant for you and me today. This passage begins by addressing the wife and her relationship to her husband. Sometimes the wife is living for God, but the husband is doing his own thing away from God. In this kind of situation, does the wife have to be submissive to her husband? The answer to that is yes, unless her husband is asking her to do something that is contrary to the Word of God. Scripture verifies that her submissive and godly spirit has the power to win her husband to Christ and His ways. A godly wife's behavior has the power to make a difference in her family.

God's Word advocates that the hidden person of a woman's heart is very important, not just her external appearance. Women should strive to have the imperishable quality of a gentle and quiet spirit, which God says is very precious in His sight. Contemporary American culture is totally against this kind of thinking. The culture today promotes the outward appearance of women, much to the exclusion of their inward beauty. Christian women today must be countercultural in their womanhood.

The mark of a holy woman is that she adorns herself by submitting to her husband and resting in his leadership. Her husband is to bring her so much security that she rests not only beside him, but in him. This will cease any fear in the life of a woman.

For those of you who are married women, do you adorn yourself by submitting to your husband and resting in his leadership? Do you spend more time working on your inward beauty than you do your outward beauty? Is your spirit controlled by gentleness? These scriptures speak to some very delicate issues in the lives of women today. Be willing to be countercultural. Do not let your culture determine what you should be, but let God's Word show you the characteristics of a real godly woman.

In this same manner, the husband is to live with his wife in an understanding way. Sensitivity toward his wife should be the husband's number one agenda. Since his wife does not usually have the physical strength to overcome him, the husband needs to be gentle to her, understanding that he is to be the spiritual leader of the family. The Bible urges the husband to honor his wife because she has experienced the grace of God in the same manner as her husband. In order for a man to honor his wife, he has to show her that she is a very valuable asset to him. He must treat her as special and worthy of honor.

This is very difficult for men because of our sinful nature and sinful choices. Most men do not have a healthy view of their wives. They distort verses like this one and try to use it for their advantage. This is very unfortunate because God intends for the husband to cherish and protect his wife. If you are a husband, be sensitive to your wife. Honor her at all times.

One phrase in this Scripture is particularly important for any Spirit-controlled believer, male or female: "so that your prayers may not be hindered." Husbands must fulfill their biblical role, and wives must fulfill their biblical role. If this occurs, harmony will take place. If they fail to fulfill their divinely designed roles, then the Bible clearly states that their prayers will be hindered.

One phrase in this Scripture is particularly important for any Spirit-controlled believer, male or female: "so that your prayers may not be hindered." If they fail to fulfill their divinely designed roles, then the Bible clearly states that their prayers will be hindered.

The great Bible scholar and teacher Warren Wiersbe has a great insight about this word *hindered*. He writes:

> The word *hindered* has an interesting meaning in the original. It means to break up a road so that the army can't get through. In ancient warfare, this method was often used. The soldiers would block the road with rocks, trees and other barriers to prevent the opposing army from advancing. Thus, 1 Peter 3:7 is telling husbands and wives that if they are not getting along with each other, their prayers will be hindered. They will be putting up barricades and barriers along the road that will prevent God from answering their prayers.[2]

The most special human relationship on this earth is the relationship between husband and wife.

One of the main reasons that many of you feel that your prayers never get above the ceiling is because of your relationship with your spouse. God calls women to live verses 1–6 so their prayers will not be hindered. He calls men to live verse 7 so that their prayers will not be hindered.

Notice the word picture of the word *hindered* described by Warren Wiersbe. When a husband and a wife do not get along, they will put up a wall between themselves that will inevitably result in unanswered prayer.

These verses put forth a very piercing, penetrating, and convicting principle for all persons who really want to be all that God has intended them to be in life: The way you treat your spouse will determine the way God treats your prayers. If you and your spouse are not enjoying intimacy in your relationship, then you will not see your prayers answered. Let me repeat: The way you treat your spouse will determine the way God treats your prayers. How are you treating your spouse? Is your relationship intimate every day or just when you have the hots for one another?

In my first pastorate, Jeana and I would leave our college setting and drive on Sunday mornings to our ministry. We had just been married, and the challenges were great as Jeana had just completed her degree and was working full-time. I was one year away from finishing my degree, so I was going to school full-time and pastoring this church on weekends.

One Sunday morning, Jeana and I had a disagreement that resulted in a fellowship problem between us. I went back to my "office" (actually, the janitor's closet) to pray before Sunday school, but I sensed that something just wasn't right. I was convicted by the Holy Spirit that I needed to be reconciled with Jeana. God would not anoint me for the morning until I made things right with my wife.

I went to the auditorium where Jeana was sitting in preparation for worship. I took her aside and repented for my words spoken to her that morning. She repented of her part of the disagreement. Then the Lord was faithful to anoint us for the day.

I learned through that experience that Satan will do all he can to damage my relationship with my wife because that strained relationship would greatly affect my relationship with God. Therefore, Jeana and I made a covenant not to come close to disagreement on Sundays about anything ever again. God has truly honored this covenant during the years.

While intimacy with your spouse will determine your intimacy with God, it is important to realize that intimacy with God will determine your intimacy with your spouse. Both must take place or else intimacy will not occur—in other words, your prayers will go unanswered.

Praying together with your family will create accountability for everyone in the family unit. It is difficult to hold a grudge with a person you are praying with regularly. Intimacy within the entire family will not occur without times of prayer with the family. The way you treat the members of your family will determine the way God treats your prayers.

Are things becoming clearer for you now? Are you understanding why you do not have intimacy in your family? Are you beginning to understand why many of your prayers go unanswered by the Lord? The wall of strained relationships must come down before your prayers go up.

Actions That Will Bring the Wall Down

If a wall is built up between you and God because of strained relationships, there are some actions you can take that will bring the wall down. I want to identify two actions you can take that will bring down this wall . . .

The First Move Is Always Yours

If there is a strained or even broken relationship in your life, the first move is always yours. It does not matter who is at fault. It is never easy to make the first move. Periodically you may get into the "if only" game. You say, "If only my wife would" or, "If only this guy in the church would" or, "If only my children would." These statements are senseless. It does not matter what anyone else does. What matters is what you are doing to bring the relationship into total purity and unity. Jesus does not want to do business with you until you have things right with other people. The first move is always yours.

There have been many times in relationships when I have sensed someone was being guarded with me. This usually comes because they feel that I have offended them in some way. I used to wait for people to come to me, but that rarely happened. I decided to fulfill Scripture, so now I go to other people when I think an offense has occurred. This humble act of making the first move has proved to be a spiritual example for them to follow.

Remember, the first move is always yours. You do as much as you can to make sure you are at peace with all people.

Be a Bridge, Not a Barrier

Many Christians have become very discouraged through friendly fire. Some Christians are like guerrilla-warfare believers who blow up bridges with the intention of helping things out. God is not in the business of alienating the world but reconciling the world unto Himself.

Build bridges with other people. This can serve as a way to win them to Christ or to win them over to walk in the ways of Christ.

In your relationships with other people, be a bridge, not a barrier.[3] Do whatever it takes to build bridges with people. Try to keep things right with them. Go the extra mile with them so you can possibly experience oneness with them. Your flesh may have to die in order to build a bridge with others. Periodically, your flesh may cause you to think you would rather blow up the bridge by walking away from the relationship and declaring that it is of no value. Do not do this! Build bridges with other people. This can serve as a way to win them to Christ or to win them over to walk in the ways of Christ.

These two actions will bring down the walls between you and others and the wall that may appear to be between you and God.

Choose to make the first move. It is always your move! Choose to build bridges with people. This is the way love can travel. It cannot travel apart from the tracks of a relationship. Do what you can to make the relationship successful.

A Major Sin in the Body of Christ

On a few occasions I have been asked, "Dr. Floyd, what do you see as the major sin in the body of Christ?" I believe that one of the major sins in the body of Christ is the sin of unforgiveness. It is amazing that the same people who have experienced God's amazing grace have the greatest struggle to forgive others when they are wronged. Unforgiveness in your heart will quench the possibility for your prayers to be answered.

This is why it is important that you make the first move. Never let resentment or unforgiveness lodge in your heart for any length of time or else you will hinder your spiritual growth. It takes a committed person to build bridges with people. Anyone can blow them up!

The wall of strained relationships must come down before your prayers go up. Consider the following two statements as you deal with any strained relationships you have in your life:

1. Your vertical relationship with God will determine your horizontal relationships with people.

2. Your horizontal relationships with people will determine your vertical relationship with God.

The two relationships go hand in hand. Your relationships with people will be affected by your relationship with God. You do not treat people in the right way when your relationship with God is not going too well. In the same way, your relationships with other people will affect your relationship with God. If things are not going well with others, then do not expect to do any serious praying business with God. Remember, the way you treat others will determine how God treats your prayers.

What is God saying to you through this chapter? I hope you will evaluate this chapter thoroughly. This is one of the most pivotal walls that must come down if God is going to hear and answer your prayers.

Do whatever it takes to make things right with other people. Take actions now toward reconciliation. Not tomorrow, but today. Do whatever it takes to make things right with God. It is urgent to do business with God. He is waiting on you to do business with Him. Whatever the cost, be right with God and with others so that your prayers will be answered.

Chapter 13

The Wall of Improper Motives

One of the great joys of my life has been serving as a pastor of a local church. I have seen many changes occur in my twenty-two years of pastoral ministry. Within the last seven years, the changes have been rapid and frightening.

When I first began pastoring, people had a great love for the local church. The church was the source of strength for people. The church had great respect in the community. The pastor of the church was usually a highly respected leader in the community. People gave time to serve the Lord through their local church. The church was driven to help those who were truly in need, especially those who did not know Christ in a personal way.

Now, twenty-two years later, the landscape of the local church has greatly changed. The church may be just one of many spiritual stops for a believer to gain strength. Few churches in our society today are respected by the community. It is highly unusual for the community even to know the pastor of a local church, much less respect him for the calling of God in his life. People give little time, if any, to serve the Lord through their local church. Today, the church is usually driven to meet the needs of its own members, rather than the needs of unbelievers.

I believe one of the most distinct changes during my twenty-two years of pastoral ministry has to do with the motives of people. No one truly knows the motives of another person. Yet, it is very obvious that, in a general way, the vast majority of Christians have experienced a major realignment of their motives. It is very rare to see a Christian in today's culture who is motivated to serve others before he has his own needs met.

The church culture of today reflects the consumer-driven mentality of America. The number one priority of most church members is, "What are you doing to meet my needs?" Their goal is not to serve the Lord through serving others but to have their needs met by others. If a Christian does not have his needs met in a church, then he will just move on to greener pastures.

It is like the old service-station concept. Christians pull into the church. They sit in their car. They are waited on in every way. Then they drive away, only to return when they need help again. If the service does not meet their expectations, then they just change service stations.

This is the secular church in our day. Christians come to worship at a church out of personal need rather than personal conviction. Their goal is to have their needs met. The thought of others rarely enters their mind. If the church they have attended for years ceases to meet their needs, then they change the place where they receive service. The end result of this entire episode is that most Christians believe that the church exists solely for the purpose of meeting their personal needs.

The way Christians relate to the church today illustrates one of the most distinct hindrances to prayer. I am convinced that there are some walls that must come down before your prayers go up. One of the great barriers to prayer is the wall of improper motives. When you go to God in prayer with improper motives, your prayers will not be productive.

What is happening in today's church mirrors what is happening in the hearts of Christians. This "serve me" mentality is reflected in the way people pray. Their view of God is very limited. They see Him as a spiritual Santa Claus who exists only to meet their needs. The problem with that view of God is that people will tend to give up on God, just like they give up on their local church if their needs are not met according to their expectations.

Let me get something straight right now. God is sovereign. He is the supreme rank and rule in the entire universe. He has absolutely no need for us because He is God. God is holy. He cannot look upon sin. God is omnipotent. He can do anything at anytime and can do it anywhere He chooses. God is omnipresent. God is everywhere. God is omniscient. He knows everything about us, including our motives.

The bottom line is that you cannot play games with God. He is all. He has all. He knows all. What a God!

It would be helpful for you to think upon the omniscience of God. You cannot hide anything from Him. Remember, He knows everything about you, including your motives. You cannot pretend to pray in an unselfish way when your heart is filled with improper motives because God looks upon your heart. He is not impressed with the words you say to Him when your heart is not right. The bottom line is that you cannot play games with God. He is all. He has all. He knows all. What a God!

Is There a Word from the Lord about Improper Motives?

A motive expresses the reality of what is in your heart and who you really are in life. A motive shares why you do what you do in your life. No line of cosmetics can cover up the truth of why you do what you do in your life.

The American culture is very performance based. Our culture tends to judge just about everything on the basis of what is done and how it is done. If the numbers are not there in regard to expected production, then you are regarded as a loser. If you do not have more wins than losses, then people start to question your ability. These things, however, are not always a proper measurement of value.

God's primary concern is not, "What have you done lately for Me?" The key question in the mind of God is, "Why do you do what you do for Me?" One day you will be judged not only for what you have done in your Christian life, but for why you have done what you have done. The "why" will usually determine the "what." You need to be much more focused on why you do something, rather than on what you have chosen to do.

Yes, there is a word from the Lord about improper motives. James 4:3 says, "You ask and do not receive, because you ask with wrong motives, so that you may spend it on your pleasures." The Bible says that the prayers of these believers were unanswered because their motives were improper.

When these Christians bowed to pray, they did not have the right heart. They never dealt with the critical question of, "Why am I praying for this?" They were probably so involved in expressing their requests to God that they never slowed down long enough to let Him talk to them about the condition of their hearts.

The Bible calls these selfish motives evil. When you pray selfishly, you are praying in an evil manner. When you lift up yourself in prayer, you are praying in an evil manner.

The purpose of prayer is never getting your way or having your needs met. The purpose of prayer is always seeking God's will. One of the reasons you are commanded to pray is to get in on what God is doing around you. If you spend all your time asking God to meet your needs, then you will miss the real issue of prayer. You will see prayer as a frustrating spiritual exercise when God does not answer.

The problem in the lives of the Christians in James 4:3 is they were asking for things with the wrong motives. God does not mind your making personal requests in prayer. After all, He wants to meet your needs. But He doesn't like for you to make your requests for the purpose of selfish gain. God is not pleased when your prayers are spent on your own pleasures.

Prayer is to be a holy time of communication with God. Prayer is a very special time with God. It is an act of true worship. All of your desires and pleasures need to be laid aside. Remember, praying is about God's will being done, not your will.

Some translations of James 4:3 use the word *pleasures,* and others translate the word as *lusts.* A very good explanation of this text is as follows: "Lust is anything for which we have a strong desire. James chose the word *hedone* in Greek for this idea. You don't have to be a rocket scientist to see a close English derivative: *hedonism,* the belief that pleasure or happiness is the sole goal of life. . . . Praying for God to give you something for no purpose other than your hedonistic pleasure is a sure way to have your prayers fall on deaf ears."[1] This is a very sobering commentary on this verse.

The American culture is committed to the god of hedonism. At times, the church even commits adultery with this god. When you understand James 4:3, you begin to realize how far off base we are in our prayers. We have squandered many of our prayers on a belief system that says pleasure or happiness is the sole goal of life. This is hedonism, not biblical Christianity.

Hedonism declares that the goal of your life should be making sure your own pleasures are met with the ultimate outcome being your own personal happiness. Christianity declares that the goal of your life is bringing glory to God by pleasing Him in everything you do. Many times this has nothing to do with your needs being met or your pleasures being experienced.

When you pray for selfish motives in your heart so that your life can be more filled with pleasure or happiness, you have missed God's heart for prayer. When you choose to spend your prayers on your own pleasures, then you are disregarding God's will.

America is a country that is consumed with self-gratification. This hedonistic mentality has invaded the church of Jesus Christ. Christians have been so deceived by Satan that they have adopted the philosophy and practice of hedonism and brought it into the church. This is why the main agenda of most Christians is their personal happiness, which they think is possible only when their needs are met. This is very tragic, and it breaks the heart of God.

This wall in prayer is why the church is so powerless today. When Christians and their churches buy into this vain pagan philosophy, they have exchanged the truth for a lie. Since God knows everything He is aware of the intents and the motives of each person. When God sees that a person's motives for prayer have been polluted by this unbiblical mentality, then He does not answer that person's prayer.

It is time to check your motives in prayer. One day in the future God will reveal all of your motives in life: "For God will bring every act to judgment, everything which is hidden, whether it is good or evil" (Eccles. 12:14).

Jesus reaffirms that everything you do will be made known: "But you, when you pray, go into your inner room, and when you have shut your door, pray to your Father who is in secret, and your Father who sees in secret will repay you" (Matt. 6:6).

This emphasis on your motives being revealed is affirmed again in Hebrews 4:13: "There is no creature hidden from His sight, but all things are open and laid bare to the eyes of Him with whom we have to do."

Nothing and no one in creation is hidden from God. One day everything and everyone will be laid bare before the Lord. All will give an account to Him. You will not one day stand before a jury of men concerning your motives. You will one day stand before God Himself. In this setting you will give an account of your life to Him. Juries of men make mistakes, but God never makes a mistake. You could hide your motives from a jury of men, but you will not be able to hide any motives from the all-knowing, holy God.

> You could hide your motives from a jury of men, but you will not be able to hide any motives from the all-knowing, holy God.

God always knows your motives when you pray. God always knows what you are up to in your life. When your motives are not right, then God will not answer your prayer. This wall of improper motives must come down before your prayers go up.

Does this mean that it is wrong to pray for your needs to be met? Absolutely not! It is only wrong when you pray with the improper motive that disregards the will of God in order to accomplish your own will. This sovereign and holy God is not your puppet who stands ready to respond to you when you choose to pray some cute prayer. The Father cannot be manipulated. Your will is not the issue. The will of the Father is always the highest concern in prayer.

There is a word from the Lord about having improper motives in prayer. The word about this subject is not gentle but very firm. If we pray the way God wants us to pray, the walls will come down and our prayer lives will be very effective. Productive praying will happen when you check your motives in prayer.

How to Check Your Motives in Prayer

Since your goal is to be an effective prayer warrior, then you must make sure that your motives are right. I want to give you three questions to ask yourself when you pray that will check your motives in prayer. The first question is . . .

Why Am I Asking God for This?

For the next several days, present your requests to God in prayer. Then ask, "Why am I asking God for this?" The heart of the issue in prayer is not *what* you are asking for as much as it is *why* you are asking God for this.

Are you asking God for something in prayer so that your will can be accomplished in the situation? Are you asking God for something in prayer so that your needs will be met? Are you asking God for something in prayer because you think you will be more happy if you receive it? Could it be that you are asking God for something in prayer because you know if He answers that prayer you will receive all the glory for it?

I guarantee you that the issue of why you are asking God for something in prayer will be one of the biggest struggles you will face in your prayer life. Even as a prayer veteran, I still struggle with this issue. Remember the dilemma I mentioned in chapter 8 about getting my first book published? God didn't answer my prayers initially because I was asking for purely selfish reasons. Once I was able to pray with pure motives, agreeing to let God receive all the glory for any published book, He answered my prayers and the book was published. A Christian who operates with the highest level of integrity will want his prayer life to be pure.

This question, "Why am I asking God for this?" is a question that cuts to the quick. If you will ask yourself this question when you pray, you will be more likely to have pure motives in prayer. The ultimate result will be that your prayers will be answered.

Another question that you should ask yourself in prayer in order to check your motives is . . .

Am I Willing to Lay Aside My Will So That God's Will Can Be Done?

This question has the power to show you how much of a mess your prayer life is probably in today. When you ask yourself this question, you will find out just how warped your views of God and prayer have become. In addition, you may discover some things about yourself that you may not want to talk about with anyone except God.

The next time you are really baring your heart to God in prayer about something, stop for a moment and give yourself a motive check. After you ask, "Why am I praying this prayer?" go another step and ask, "Am I willing to lay aside my will so that God's will can be done?" Jesus is very clear that prayer should always be not my will but God's will be done. Personally, I am very pleased that God does not let my will determine my prayers. If He did, my life would probably be in chaos heading for destruction.

Your goal in prayer should not be for the Lord to meet your needs so that you can have a better life. Your goal in prayer should be, "God, I only want it done if it will please You." Sometimes God may give you what you want, then you wake up and realize that it was really not important at all. Are you willing to set aside your agenda in prayer and exchange it for God's agenda for your life?

Personally, I am very pleased that God
does not let my will determine my prayers.
If He did, my life would probably be in
chaos heading for destruction.

There are times in your prayer life when you need to set aside your plan for prayer. You need to get on your knees before God, with your Bible open, and tell God that you want to pray according to His will about everything. Lean on Him to help you pray in the Spirit as you were taught to do in chapter 6. Do you know what will happen when you do this? God will dictate the next few minutes of your prayer life, rather than you and your selfish desires. The end result is that you will pray according to His will and your prayers will be productive.

God makes His will known to you through His Word. God energizes His Word. He does not energize your words. This is why you must be willing to lay aside your will so that God's will may be done. I can assure you that this veteran of prayer still struggles in this area of prayer. As much as I want God's will in my life and do not want to live away from His will in prayer, I still struggle with laying aside my will.

Sometimes it is just hard to discern your own will from God's will. Hopefully, most of the time they are one. In prayer they had better be one, or else your prayers will go unanswered.

There is one other question that will help you check your motives in prayer . . .

Is My Main Concern That God Get the Glory for It?

Is your concern in prayer that you get this prayer answered because you really need it answered or is it because you want God to get the glory for answering it? God is a way-maker when you get desperate enough that you want Him to get the glory for what is done. God does not make ways for proud, self-sufficient, and hedonistic Christians; He makes a way for people who come to Him with a pure heart and pure motives.

Your heart should be that if your request pleases the Father, then you want God to do it. After all, if it does not please the Father, why in the world would you want God to do it? You see, God wants the glory for your life. He will not share His glory with anyone. The number one competitor to the glory of God is your glory.

The number one goal in your prayers must be that God would receive the glory for the requests you make and for the answers He provides. Your heart needs to be like this: "Lord, if it will bring You glory to do what I have asked You, then I pray that You will do it. If the request does not bring You glory, then, Lord, please disregard it." When you have completed your prayer requests the next time you pray, conclude your prayer time with the following prayer:

Lord, with the requests I have made of You today, only give me what brings glory to You. I have laid all of this stuff before You. I need You to get involved in these matters and for You to operate in my life. You know at times I am selfish and proud. At times, I do not even know the difference between what is right and what is wrong. Therefore, protect me from myself so that You alone would receive glory. Give to me today only what will bring You glory, God.

This is a very important prayer. If you will bare your heart to God like that, He will be your way-maker. He will take away all the walls of prayer so that perfect peace will be set upon your heart in all things.

When you pray in this manner, your desires will become the desires of God. As the psalmist said, "Delight yourself in the LORD; and He will give you the desires of your heart" (37:4). One of the ways you can delight in the Lord is to delight in His will for your life. When this occurs, the result will be that your desire will become God's desire for your life. At this point, God will energize your will to become His will. This is what brings God glory.

Ask yourself these three questions when you pray and you will develop motives that are pure. The result will be answered prayer that brings God great glory!

A Final Word

I want to close this chapter by presenting to you a passage of Scripture:

According to the grace of God which was given to me, as a wise master builder I laid a foundation, and another is building upon it. But let each man be careful how he builds upon it. For no man can lay a foundation other than the one which is laid, which is Jesus Christ. Now if any man builds upon the foundation with gold, silver, precious stones, wood, hay, straw, each man's work will become evident; for the day will show it, because it is to be revealed with fire; and the fire itself will test the quality of each man's work. If any man's work which he has built upon it remains, he shall receive a reward. If any man's work is burned up, he shall suffer loss; but he himself shall be saved, yet so as through fire. (1 Cor. 3:10–15)

This is a passage about the judgment seat of Jesus Christ, when all Christians will stand before the Lord and answer to God for their lives. This judgment is not to determine eternal salvation; as a Christian, all your sins were once and for all judged at the cross and wiped away forever. The judgment seat of Christ will determine the amount of rewards in heaven that each Christian will receive.

Everything that you have done in your Christian life will be judged by fire. Every work you have built for the Lord will be judged. This time of judgment will judge the quality of your work for the Lord while you are here on earth. What does this mean?

This means that what you have done for the Lord and why you have done what you have done for the Lord will be judged. Please notice that why you have done what you have done will have as much value as what you have done for the Lord. Rewards will be given in heaven not for what you do but for what you do with the right motive.

The wall of improper motives must come down before your prayers go up. Check your motives. Just as an experienced airline pilot goes through his detailed checklist before takeoff, you need to go through the three questions on the checklist I have given you in this chapter each time you pray. Even though the pilot is experienced in flying, he does not negate the need to go through the checklist prior to his departure. Likewise, even though you may be a prayer veteran, you need to check your motives daily. God energizes your prayers when you pray with a heart that has no improper motives. The ultimate result of such purehearted praying is answered prayer.

Chapter 14

THE WALL OF AN
UNREPENTANT HEART

Many years ago, home architecture created the wave of building "shotgun houses." This simple architecture acquired its name because you could open the front door of the house and see all the way through the house, peering even through the back door. If you took a shotgun and shot at the front door, nothing would stand in its way as the blast traveled all the way through the back door of the house.

Your grandmother may have had a house like this. As you would walk through the hallway toward the back of the house, you would see numerous doors off of the hallway, opening into several rooms, such as a kitchen, living room, bedrooms, and a bathroom. The doors to these rooms would all be open—except one door. If you happened to be a guest in that house, you might be tempted to open the one door that was shut. But if you placed your hand on that door to open it, the woman of the house would say, "Do not dare go into that room. That is my junk room." Each room of the house would be clean except for the junk room. Therefore, this room was off-limits to all guests.

Is your heart in the same condition as what is described in these shotgun houses? Perhaps most of the rooms of your heart are clean and presentable, but is there a junk room in your heart? Are you afraid to let anyone enter that room and see its condition? Most likely, you would be embarrassed for others to know what is inside the junk room in your heart. That room may contain some passions, desires, vain imaginations, speculations, and secret sins that you have lived with so long that you are not sure you are willing to live without.

Just as keeping the door closed to the junk room of the house does not eliminate the junk, not dealing with the junk in your heart does not eliminate it. This chapter is about the secret sins of your life—the kind of sins that you would be ashamed of if others knew about them. These secret sins in your heart are like bricks that are used to build a wall—a wall that keeps your prayer life from being effective. This wall built by the secret sins of your heart must come down for your prayers to go up.

> This chapter is about the secret sins of your life—the kind of sins that you would be ashamed of if others knew about them.

The Bible teaches that sin should never be cherished in the life of those who follow God. Psalm 66:18 says, "If I regard wickedness in my heart, the Lord will not hear." The word *regard* in this verse can also be translated as *cherish*. So it could read, "If I *cherish* wickedness in my heart . . ." This is the Hebrew word *rasah,* which means "to approve of, to enjoy, and to show respect for something." I really like what Woodrow Kroll writes about this: "If we are enjoying sin and praying to God at the same time, we are showing more respect to sin than to God. God is under no obligation to listen to prayers that come from disrespectful hearts. If we approve of something we know is wrong and attempt to talk with God at the same time, we might as well save our breath."[1] This is a strong word based on the Word of God.

The Scriptures say to you that if you cherish or approve of sin in your life, the Lord will not hear your prayers. I mentioned in chapter 12 that I once tried to pray for God's anointing on my ministry while I was holding on to the sin of an unrepentant heart toward my wife. At first, I didn't want to apologize to her for the disagreement we had had on the way to church. Because of my unrepentant heart, God did not hear my prayer. I knew I needed to repent or God would not anoint me with His Holy Spirit as I preached that day. It was not until I confessed my unforgiveness to God and then truly repented to Jeana that God prepared us for ministry that day.

Is there something in your heart that you really love but know that it is just not right? Is there something in your junk room that you know needs to be thrown out of your life, but at this time you have just not dealt with the problem? This sin may be something that is very private. It is something that you do not want others to know. According to the Scriptures, God will not hear the prayer of a Christian who is willingly holding on to sin in his or her life.

When you choose to hang on to your sin, your heart is unrepentant. The word *repent* means to have a change of mind about your sin. Therefore, if you are unrepentant, you have not changed your mind about your sin. Instead, you accommodate your sin. You cherish your sin. You are hospitable to the sin in your heart. The result is that your unrepentant heart becomes a wall between you and God.

The Connection Principle

I believe there is a principle that is aligned with the teaching of Psalm 66:18. I am calling this principle the connection principle. Stated simply: **All prayer, to be acceptable to God, must be connected with a purpose to forsake all sin.** Prayer connects you to God and gives you the joy of talking to God. You connect with God for the purpose of keeping your life on the right path. But if you truly desire to be on the right path in your life, you must forsake all sin.

If you are going to connect with God, you must forsake all sin in your life. This divine connection does not permit evil to interrupt the connection. It is important to remember that God is very concerned about your attitude toward your sin. For you to kneel and pray without forsaking sin in your heart is like attempting spiritual exercise without getting any results.

Repentance involves abandoning sin in your heart when you pray. Repentance is forsaking all sin, including the secret sins, for the purpose of connecting with God and communicating with Him. Do you want God to speak to you when you pray? Do you want God to empower you when you pray? These things will only happen as you forsake all sin by connecting with God.

Secret sin has a way of settling into your heart. Would you be embarrassed if all the rooms of your heart were exposed to everyone? Let me remind you that God knows the content of every room in your heart. What is the secret sin of your life? Is there any degree of pornography in your life? Perhaps pornography began to invade your life as a child. Through the years, a stronghold of sensuality and sexuality has turned into a fatal attraction in your life. Is there any level of unforgiveness in your life? Perhaps you hold a grudge toward someone that has now lodged itself deep into the junk room of your life. You know that you should not live with this, but you are having a hard time letting it go because it gratifies you to resent the person. Are you stealing from God with the resources God has entrusted to you? God has asked you to honor Him by giving a portion of all your resources to your local church. Your greed and personal drive for satisfaction have kept this from coming to an end in your life. Are you struggling with lusts in your life? The persons you work with serve as a field for lusting after persons of the opposite sex. Perhaps a few might be reading this book who struggle with lusting after a person of the same gender. Yet a desire to cherish sin will result in your prayers not going up to God. If your prayers are going to be acceptable to God, then you need to forsake all sin in your life.

Would you let the Holy Spirit clean out the junk room of your heart? He will ensure that you no longer tolerate these sins. In addition to allowing the Holy Spirit to be involved in your life, submit yourself to another person who can make you accountable for what has been piled up in your heart's junk room. This person must be willing to speak the truth to you in love.

You see, the connection principle teaches you that the secret sins of your life must be forsaken for your prayers to be acceptable to God. You can pray, shout, clap your hands, raise your hands, witness, sing, and even preach. But if you do any of these things while cherishing sin in your heart, God will neither hear your prayers nor accept your worship. The wall of an unrepentant heart must come down before God will answer your prayers.

Is your heart unrepentant? I want to give to you some . . .

Symptoms of an Unrepentant Heart

There are certain physical symptoms that may tell you when you have heart trouble. These symptoms are not the main problem, though you may initially think so. These symptoms reveal that you have a problem with your heart. A proper medical diagnosis will determine what needs to be done in order for your heart problem to be solved.

Just as this is true for the human heart in relation to physical health, it is also true for the spiritual heart in relationship to your spiritual condition. I want to share with you four symptoms that indicate that you may have a problem with an unrepentant heart. The first symptom is that an unrepentant heart . . .

Keeps on Sinning

When your heart is unrepentant, you just keep on sinning. You continue to give in to your sinful nature and desires. Your life is ruled more by sin than by righteousness. You have a passion to fulfill the sinful desires of your flesh, not a serious desire to neglect them. As a result, you just keep on sinning.

A man who claims to be a Christian has a real problem with extreme lusts. In spite of the fact that his lusts have resulted in several adulterous relationships, he attends church on a weekly basis. His involvement in Sunday school has turned into an opportunity to pursue other women. When confronted, he always denies his sinful behavior. Yet he continues committing adultery.

This man's problem is that his heart is unrepentant. He just keeps on sinning. If he never repents from his sin, he is probably lost spiritually. If he knows Christ, he will be under severe judgment in his life. The sad commentary on this man's life is that he has just never gotten over this problem.

Do you keep on sinning in your life?
If so, you have an unrepentant heart.
God wants you to repent.

Lusts and adultery are not his problems; they are merely the symptoms of his problem. His problem is that he has an unrepentant heart. This is evidenced because he keeps on sinning.

Do you keep on sinning in your life? If so, you have an unrepentant heart. God wants you to repent. He wants you to forsake sin, not embrace it. A person with an unrepentant heart keeps on sinning, but a person with an unrepentant heart also . . .

Ignores God's Convicting Spirit about the Sin

Every true follower of Jesus Christ is indwelt by the Holy Spirit of God. He is there to assist and empower you, but He is also there to convict you of sin in your life. Therefore, whenever you sin, the Holy Spirit will show you that you have sinned and convict you that you have done wrong.

If your heart is unrepentant, then you will choose to ignore the conviction of God's Spirit in your life when you sin. This unrepentant heart chooses to take life into its own hands. It is a dangerous place to be in life.

My wife, Jeana, has the gift of mercy. I remember one time when she decided to take up an offense for me and confronted a person about something. This needed to done, but she was not the person to do it. After the confrontation, the Lord kept her up all night. When I awakened that morning, she was under major conviction from God for this action, which I interpreted as being a minor issue. As soon as she could call that person to make things right through repentance, she did so.

You see, Jeana had a repentant heart. I commend her for her extreme sensitivity to the Holy Spirit. She responded to His conviction as every Christian should respond to the Holy Spirit. She recognized her sin. She dealt with her sin. She repented of her sin. She made restitution for her sin. This story has always been a great model to me of how each Christian should respond to the Holy Spirit when He convicts us of our sin.

Jeana is an example of a repentant heart. Do you have a repentant heart? An unrepentant heart ignores God's convicting Spirit toward sin. When God convicts you of sin in your life, repent of it. Do not ignore the Holy Spirit's conviction.

A person who has an unrepentant heart continues to sin and ignores God's Spirit when He convicts them of sin they have committed. Another mark of an unrepentant heart is that it . . .

Turns into a Hard Heart

You enter a dangerous zone in your spiritual life when you let your heart become unrepentant. Repentance does not end at salvation; repentance begins at salvation.

When you ignore the conviction of the Holy Spirit toward the sin in your life, you will develop a hard heart. When your heart becomes hard, your personality changes. Your countenance changes. Everything about you changes. You do not see things the way you need to see them. Your life becomes somewhat blurred.

Remember this: Once you reject the Holy Spirit's conviction upon your life, it will become easier to say no to Him again. Why? Because your heart is being hardened. Saying no to God's conviction in your life is dangerous. Once your heart is hardened, sinning will become more of a way of life for you.

An unrepentant heart keeps on sinning, ignores God's convicting Spirit about the sin, turns into a hard heart, and . . .

Is More Interested in Learning How to Manage Sin Effectively Than Learning How to Overcome Sin Victoriously

During the last three years, I have had the opportunity to meet many Christians from all different types of theological persuasions. I have preached in several different settings, including regional Awaken America rallies. These rallies are for believers in Christ who desire to see revival and spiritual awakening in their region. Several churches come together to worship and be challenged together from God's Word.

In these travels I have been able to learn so much. Along with these opportunities and others, I have discerned something very disturbing that is taking place in Christianity—that is, the symptom of an unrepentant heart.

Most of the Christians I have met across America seem to be more interested in learning how to manage their sin effectively than they are in learning how to overcome their sin victoriously. Most Christians just want to make sure they do not get caught in their sin. They want to make sure that they can enjoy their sin and not have to pay too heavy of a price for it. Therefore, their goal is to manage their sin, not to overcome it.

This symptom is dangerous and deceitful. I want to warn you not to let your spiritual life get that warped. Do not become deceived. Your goal as a growing Christian should be to overcome your sin, not just manage it more effectively.

Remember that an unrepentant heart will keep your prayers from being answered. I know you want to have a repentant heart. Therefore it is time to . . .

Clean the Junk from Your Heart

Can you pray in the Spirit if you cherish sin? Can you pray in faith if you cherish sin? Can you pray with passion, fire, and conviction if you cherish sin? Can you do serious warfare praying and cherish sin? The answer to those questions is the same: No!

If you cherish sin, your spiritual life will eventually become dull and heavy. The things that used to bother you will no longer bother you because your heart will have hardened. This hard heart will grease the slide for Satan to take you deeper into sin. When you cherish sin, you stop expecting God to work in your life.

Would you take some time right now and look into that junk room of your life? Do not keep it off-limits from the Holy Spirit. Do not let things pile up to such a point that you do not even know what is in there. Deal with the secret sins of your life. Now is the time to clean the junk out of your heart.

> Would you take some time right now and look into that junk room of your life? Do not keep it off-limits from the Holy Spirit.

In just a moment would you take the time to investigate seriously what is in that private room of your heart? Would you let the Lord show you what is in there that does not please Him? Would you respond to His Spirit when He shows you that there are some things that you have held on to for years that do not need to be in your life? It is time to clean out the junk.

During these next few moments, take the time to evaluate what might be in the junk room of your heart. This inventory calls you into being honest with God and with yourself. Evaluate your junk room with the following scriptures and questions:

1. In everything give thanks; for this is the will of God in Christ Jesus for you (1 Thess. 5:18, NKJV).

Do you worry about anything? Have you forgotten to thank God for all things, the seemingly bad as well as the good? Do you neglect to give Him thanks for your breath, your health, and for life itself?

2. Now to Him who is able to do exceedingly abundantly above all that we ask or think, according to the power that works in us (Eph. 3:20, NKJV).

Do you shy away from attempting to do things in the name of your heavenly Father because you fear you are not talented enough? Do feelings of inferiority keep you from your desire to serve God? When you do accomplish something of merit, do you choose to give the glory to yourself, rather than to God?

3. You shall receive power when the Holy Spirit has come upon you; and you shall be witnesses to Me in Jerusalem, and in all Judea and Samaria, and to the end of the earth (Acts 1:8, NKJV).

Have you been hesitant to thank God for the miracles He has performed in your life? Have you been satisfied to live your Christianity in a casual manner and to think that it's not all that important to share the good news of your deliverance with others?

4. I say . . . to everyone who is among you, not to think of himself more highly than he ought to think . . . (Rom. 12:3, NKJV).

Are you overly proud of your accomplishments, your talents, or your family? Do you have difficulty putting the concerns of others first? Do you have a rebellious spirit at the thought that God may want to change you and rearrange your thinking?

5. Let all bitterness, wrath, anger, clamor, and evil speaking be put away from you, with all malice (Eph. 4:31, NKJV).

Do you complain, find fault, or argue? Do you nurse and delight in a critical spirit? Do you carry a grudge against believers of another group, denomination, or theological persuasion because they don't see the truth as you see it? Do you speak unkindly about people when they are not present? Do you find that you're often angry with yourself? With others? With God?

6. *Do you not know that your body is the temple of the Holy Spirit who is in you, whom you have from God, and you are not your own? (1 Cor. 6:19, NKJV).*

Are you careless with your body? Do you defile your body with unholy sexual acts?

7. *Let no corrupt communication proceed out of your mouth . . . (Eph. 4:29, NKJV).*

Do you use language that fails to edify others, tell off-color jokes or stories that demean another person's race, habits, or culture? Do you condone these comments when guests are in your home or when your colleagues share them with you at work?

8. *Do not . . . give place to the devil (Eph. 4:26–27, NKJV).*

Do you close your eyes to the possibility that you may be a landing strip for Satan by opening your mind to him through ungodly practices, psychic predictions, occult literature, and violent or sex-driven movies and videos? Do you seek counsel for daily living from horoscopes in the paper, on television, or on the Internet rather than from God, your true and ultimate source for living? Do you let Satan use you to set up barriers that inhibit the cause of Christ in your church and in your home through criticism and gossip?

9. *Not slothful in business . . . (Rom. 12:11, KJV).*

Are you chronically late in paying your debts, sometimes choosing not to pay them at all? Do you charge more on your credit cards than you can honestly afford to pay? Do you neglect to keep honest income-tax records? Do you engage in shady business deals?

10. *Beloved . . . abstain from fleshly lusts which war against the soul (1 Pet. 2:11, NKJV).*

Are you guilty of a lustful eye toward the opposite sex? Do you fill your mind with sexually oriented television programs, lewd movies, or unsavory books and magazines? Their covers? Centerfolds? Especially when you sense no one is watching? Do you indulge in lustful activities that God's Word condemns, such as fornication, adultery, or perversion?

11. Bearing with one another, and forgiving one another, if anyone has a complaint against another; even as Christ forgave you, so you also must do (Col. 3:13, NKJV).

Have you failed to forgive those who may have said or done something to hurt you? Have you written off certain people as not worthy of your friendship?

12. You also outwardly appear righteous to men, but inside you are full of hypocrisy and lawlessness (Matt. 23:28, NKJV).

Do you know in your heart that you are often not what people see? Are you hiding behind being active in your church as a cover for your activities away from the body of Christ? Are you mimicking the Christian faith for social status, acceptance in your church or your community? Are you real?

13. Finally, brethren, whatever things are true, whatever things are noble, whatever things are just, whatever things are pure, whatever things are lovely, whatever things are of good report, if there is any virtue and if there is anything praiseworthy—meditate on these things (Phil. 4:8, NKJV).

Do you enjoy listening to conversation that hurts others? Do you pass it on? Do you believe rumors or partial truths, especially about an enemy or a competitor? Do you choose to spend little or no time each day allowing God to speak to you through His Word?[2]

I want to challenge you to implement this chapter immediately. Find a quiet place right now. Get on your knees if you are physically able. Ask the Holy Spirit to evaluate your heart as you go through this inventory point by point. Let the Lord use this inventory to clean the junk out of your life. The result will be that God will remove the wall that keeps your prayers from going up to Him. The wall of an unrepentant heart must be abolished in order for your prayers to go up.

Section
Five

THE INFLUENCE
OF PRAYER

Chapter 15

THE INFLUENCE
OF PRAYER

Mark Brunell is one of the greatest quarterbacks in the National Football League. In his first year with the Jacksonville Jaguars, Brunell led the entire NFL in both passing and rushing yards. In addition, he was able to take every snap in that season. He was the only quarterback in the NFL to accomplish that feat.

In 1997, Mark Brunell signed a $31.5-million, five-year contract with the Jaguars. The amazing thing about Brunell is that he is only six feet tall, which is relatively short for a professional quarterback. Against all odds, Mark Brunell has made a name for himself in professional football.

Mark Brunell is an outstanding and outspoken follower of Jesus Christ. He has influenced his team in a great way. He does not live a life of compromise but a life of great conviction. Brunell has influenced the coaching staff of the Jacksonville Jaguars. When Brunell was injured in the preseason of 1997, head coach Tom Coughlin stated that he was certain that Mark knew that God had a plan for his life and for the Jacksonville Jaguars. Mark quickly overcame his injury and not only led the Jaguars to a great season, but he also influenced people all over America.

As I mentioned in chapter 7, my son Josh was a record-breaking quarterback in the history of Arkansas high school football. In 1997, Josh led his team to have the number one offense in the nation. Josh's role model as a quarterback is Mark Brunell. He identifies with him because of his commitment to Jesus Christ, as well as the challenge of performing as the quarterback of a football team. I thank God for role models like Mark Brunell, who understands that God wants to use him by influencing others through his position.

When Coach Coughlin stated that Brunell was confident that God had a plan for him and for the Jaguars, he revealed that Brunell had a tremendous commitment to prayer. Because of Brunell's prayer life, God has used him as an influential person in the sports world in America.

When prayer is prominent in your life,
you will be able to influence other people
in a significant way.

As I share with you about the influence of prayer, may I remind you how prayer can be effective? Effective prayer occurs when you talk to God and listen to what God is saying to you. The main thing in your life is that you meet with God the first thing every day. When you pray, it demonstrates that you depend on God in your life. When you do not pray, it demonstrates that you are depending upon yourself. God wants to use prayer to influence your life.

When prayer is prominent in your life, you will be able to influence other people in a significant way. One of the biblical passages that show the value of influencing others through prayer is found in Acts 16:25–34:

But about midnight Paul and Silas were praying and singing hymns of praise to God, and the prisoners were listening to them; and suddenly there came a great earthquake, so that the foundations of the prison house were shaken; and immediately all the doors were opened, and everyone's chains were unfastened. And when the jailer had been roused out of sleep and had seen the prison doors opened, he drew his sword and was about to kill himself, supposing that the prisoners had escaped. But Paul cried out with a loud voice, saying, "Do yourself no harm, for we are all here!" And he called for lights and rushed in and, trembling with fear, he fell down before Paul and Silas, and after he brought them out, he called, "Sirs, what must I do to be saved?" And they said, "Believe in the Lord Jesus, and you shall be saved, you and your household." And they spoke the word of the Lord to him together with all who were in his house. And he took them that very hour of the night and washed their wounds, and immediately he was baptized, he and all his household. And he brought them into his house and set food before them, and rejoiced greatly, having believed in God with his whole household.

The two men of God mentioned in this passage are Paul and Silas. Before Paul's conversion, he killed Christians as an occupation. After his conversion to Christianity, Paul surrendered his life to fulfill God's calling to preach the gospel to the world.

Paul and Silas were ministering in the city of Philippi. On their way to pray, they had the joy of winning Lydia and her entire family to Jesus Christ. After leading Lydia to Christ, they came across a young girl who was controlled by Satan. They stood against this demonic spirit in Jesus' name, and through warfare praying, the girl was delivered. Again on their way to pray, God used them significantly.

Once Paul and Silas had cleansed this girl, the enemies of God became angry with them. The leaders of the city arrested them, stripped them, and beat them with a rod many times. Then they threw them into prison and placed them under tight security. They took them into an inner dungeon and fastened their feet into stocks connected to the walls of the prison. All of this happened while Paul and Silas were on their way to pray. God used them in a great way, but they paid a high price to follow God.

Paul and Silas were influential men because they were men of prayer. They modeled a deep commitment to prayer, even in the midst of experiencing persecution. The American culture needs to witness men, women, teenagers, and children who are people of great influence. Just as prayer made Paul and Silas influential, prayer will make you a person of great influence. Yes, the price is high, but the reward is great. Whether you are a corporate leader, a manual laborer, a university student, or a housewife, God wants you to be a person of great influence. This influence will be determined by your prayer life. Anyone can follow the crowd. But you need to be willing to stand for God. Your stand for God is usually determined by the power of your prayer life. You can greatly influence the lives of other people through your prayers.

This is the reason why you need a plan of action in your prayer life. As I have said before, if you do not have a plan to pray, you usually will not pray. God wants to raise up countless thousands of Christians to be great prayer warriors who can influence others. Pay special attention to the next chapter as I teach you how to create your own prayer notebook.

Let's pursue other ways in which prayer can be influential.

Prayer Influences People

Paul and Silas were beaten because they loved Christ. They were placed in stocks in the inner dungeon of the prison. The Bible says that they were under tight security. I am confident that Paul and Silas would have preferred not to have been in prison. Like most people, I am sure they preferred not to experience pain. Yet at midnight, Paul and Silas began to pray and sing praises to God. The prisoners and the keepers of the prison were influenced greatly by the prayers and praises of Paul and Silas. When they began to pray, they influenced people in a positive direction toward God.

One of the greatest preachers ever to have lived was a man named Charles Haddon Spurgeon. He used to preach in London to crowds of ten thousand people. He was a man of prayer. He titled his sermon on this passage about Paul and Silas "Songs of the Night." He said that the praise and prayer of Paul and Silas were songs in the night that can only come from God, not from men.

This is so true. Nothing within Paul and Silas would have desired to be in prison, and certainly nothing in them would have desired to sing and to pray at midnight. They could have griped to God, "Lord, here we are trying to serve You and look at us—we cannot even move. They are beating us and trying to kill us. If You loved us, You would not have us go through this persecution." Yet Paul and Silas did not pray like that. Their prayers were from the divine energy within them, the Holy Spirit. As they prayed, the Spirit of God fell all over that prison. Their prayers influenced people.

How could they pray like that under such adverse circumstances? Paul and Silas were men who loved Jesus Christ more than they loved themselves. They experienced the transforming power of God in their lives. They knew what it was like to have once been spiritually lost but now found by the grace of God. They knew what it was like to have their sins forgiven and to experience the promise of heaven. They counted it as joy to suffer for Christ. This happened because they were men of prayer. Prayer influenced them, and their prayers influenced others. Their prayers were contagious.

When you are in an adverse situation like that in your life, do you pray? When others ridicule you for your faith, do you pray? Prayer can make you stand strong for God. The power of your stand will be determined by the power of your prayers. Would you become a prayer warrior and let your prayers influence other people? God wants to use you for His maximum impact, so become a person who is committed to prayer. Prayer influences people!

Prayer Influences Circumstances

When Paul and Silas prayed, God began to move in their circumstances. We do not know what they were praying about, but we do know God moved when they prayed. The Bible says the prison was shaken by God. An earthquake shook the ground and opened the prison doors. In fact, even their chains were loosened by the power of God. The jailer awakened at these supernatural events and naturally assumed that the prisoners would leave. Since he knew that he would be killed if the prisoners left under his guard, the jailer began to take actions to take his own life. When Paul observed what the jailer was about to do, he shouted at him to stop because no one had left the prison.

It is important for you to remember that God is in charge of everything. He is in charge of all circumstances. Nothing happens in your life without a purpose. When you pray, you position yourself to see what God is doing in your midst. When you pray, God will change you. He may even choose to change your circumstances. He can move miraculously and providentially.

> It is important for you to remember that God is in charge of everything. He is in charge of all circumstances. Nothing happens in your life without a purpose.

Is there anything too hard for God? Absolutely not! Prayer can change your marriage even if your marriage seems hopeless. Prayer can change what is occurring in your workplace even if your boss conducts himself like a pagan. Prayer can change your child even if she is running away from God and living in rebellion toward you. Prayer can change the doctor's diagnosis even if it is terminal. Yes, God responds to someone who depends on Him through prayer. God has the power to change your circumstances through prayer.

Have you ever looked back and wished you had changed some things in your life? Looking back, it is easy to have 20-20 vision. Yet only God can see with 20-20 vision when looking into the future. Prayer enables you to see what He sees in the midst of circumstances.

You are not hopeless. Your circumstances are not hopeless. God can change you and your circumstances through prayer.

Prayer Changes Eternity

In the midst of that prison turmoil, the jailer rushed into the cell of Paul and Silas and asked them how he could be saved. Evidently their lives had been an outstanding testimony to him. Perhaps they had witnessed to him before he fell asleep. No doubt he had heard them praying and praising God in the midst of unjust torture. When he saw that Paul and Silas could have left the cell but chose not to do so, he was astonished by this commitment.

I believe the testimony of believers would be greatly enhanced if we would respond with a positive witness for Christ through difficult circumstances. Rather than whining, we need to testify of God's greatness even in the midst of trouble. Effective praying will result in an effective witness.

This lost, pagan jailer wanted to know the Jesus that Paul and Silas knew. Paul told him that if he wanted to be saved he would have to believe in the Lord Jesus Christ only for his salvation. Paul did not tell him to go to church. Paul did not tell him to live a good life. Paul did not tell him to go and be baptized. Paul told him one simple thing: Believe on the Lord Jesus Christ and you will be saved.

In order to believe in Jesus Christ, you have to place your confidence and trust only in the Lord. You have to deny yourself by putting away your dependence upon yourself. You have to place your confidence only in the Lord. Only Jesus has the power to forgive your sins. Only Jesus has the power to give you eternal life. You cannot save yourself. Only Jesus can save you from your sins and give you the gift of eternal life.

This jailer gave his life to Jesus Christ. God used him to win his family to Jesus Christ. All of them were baptized to symbolize the new life they received in Jesus Christ. The jailer's life and the lives of his family were transformed by God's grace.

Prayer changed the eternity of these people. The prayers of Paul and Silas caught their attention. God's power fell upon them. The prayer of salvation prayed by the jailer and his family changed their eternity.

If you have come to a point in your life where you are not certain about your eternal destiny, please know that prayer can change your eternity. If you would like to settle your eternal destiny right now, would you pray the following prayer to God? If you will mean this prayer in your heart, Christ will come into your life, forgive you of your sins, and give you eternal life right now. Pray these words:

Dear Lord Jesus, I know that I am a sinner. I know that I do wrong every day of my life. I believe that You died for my sins. I believe that You were raised from the dead for me. By simple faith right now, I open the door of my heart and I ask You to come into my life right now. I rely only upon You to save me. Thank You for coming into my life right now. Thank You for taking away my sins. Thank You for giving me eternal life. Amen.

Take the time to pray that prayer, and Christ will come into your life.

When I was fifteen years old, Jesus Christ came into my life at a small Baptist church in southwest Texas. He changed me not only at salvation, but through the course of the years. Let Him come into your life right now.

Yes, prayer changes people. Prayer changes circumstances. Prayer changes eternity. Prayer is very influential. This is why you need to continue in your growth in prayer by reading and implementing a prayer plan, such as the one provided in the final chapter of this book. It is important that you do not just get more obese with spiritual knowledge like you do when you read most books. Place the truths of this book into immediate action by developing your own plan of action for prayer. If you will follow a plan of prayer, your life and the lives of others will be changed. Your circumstances may also be influenced by this plan of prayer. And yes, most important, the eternity of others can and will be influenced through this plan of prayer. Step up! Go to the next level right now in your prayer life and develop a personal prayer plan.

Chapter 16

A PERSONAL PRAYER PLAN

Prayer is a spiritual journey. Just as a journey from your present location to the other side of the country requires that you have a plan to reach your destination, you need a plan to assist you in your spiritual journey of prayer. Prayer is your personal communication with God. Since this is your spiritual destination every day, you need a plan to help you reach your destination more effectively and consistently.

I have a special plan that I want to encourage you to follow for several weeks. You can modify this plan to meet your own personal prayer needs. This chapter will teach you how to develop and use a personal prayer journal to help you along in your prayer journey.

I have been a Christian since 1971. Through all of these years, I have had seasons in which I have followed a plan to pray on a consistent basis. Conversely, for whatever reason, there have been other times when I chose not to follow a particular plan for prayer.

I have observed that the greatest times in my prayer life have been those in which I followed a specific plan of action for prayer. In these seasons I have been consistently and effectively in the presence of the

Father. You see, prayer is a journey. If I am going to reach my destination of communicating with God regularly, I need a plan that will help me get there. In this chapter, you will discover a plan that will work for you.

You should not feel that you are following someone else's plan for prayer. You should not feel bound to rules, regulations, and expectations. This plan will give you a structure where you can add the details and personal burdens of your life. This plan can be customized to fit your spiritual needs and desires.

Four Reasons That You Need to Consider Using This Prayer Plan

There are four reasons that I believe each of you needs to consider using this plan for prayer. The first reason is because it is . . .

Simple

This plan is simple for everyone to use. If a parent wanted to teach an older child to pray, he or she could use this plan. On the opposite end of the scale, if a senior adult wanted to move to another dimension in his or her prayer life, he or she could use this plan. Why can this plan span such a broad age range? Because it is a simple way to pray.

The simplicity of this plan makes it perfect for everyone. I do not like complex or complicated things. I like to keep things simple. I promise you that the plan described in this chapter will be easy for you to use in your journey of prayer. I believe if you will use it for a number of weeks, your prayer life will never be the same.

> I promise you that the plan described in this chapter will be easy for you to use in your journey of prayer.

Another reason why you should use this plan is that it is . . .

Sequential

There is a sense of order to this plan. It is a plan that is so orderly that it just makes sense. It is a plan with a sequential order that anyone can follow.

Many of you are rookies in the ministry of prayer. This may be your first attempt to establish a plan of prayer. Many of you are veterans of prayer. Perhaps you have used other plans before or you are burned out on plans of prayer. May I remind you, this plan leads you into formulating and making this plan *your plan* for prayer. Whether you are a rookie or a seasoned veteran of prayer, this plan has a place in your life.

Sometimes people design plans of prayer as if they are trying to apply a theory on prayer. This plan has been designed by a very simple-minded person who has the gift of order in his life. Simplicity combined with sequence produces relevance and productivity, particularly for followers of Christ.

Another reason you should use this plan is that it is very . . .

Specific

One of the reasons why this plan is so dynamic is that it leads you to pray for people, ministries, organizations, problems, and situations in a specific manner. Too much generalized praying is taking place today. This plan helps you to pray specifically.

The final reason that I believe this plan is worthy of your use is that it is . . .

Spiritual

This plan incorporates the Word of God into your prayer and encourages the dynamic of the Holy Spirit in the ministry of prayer. Anytime the Word of God is used and the Holy Spirit is present, something very spiritual will take place. This plan helps you see the importance of God's Word and the Holy Spirit in your communicating with God.

Therefore, you need to consider using this plan because it is a simple plan that has sequence and order. It is a plan that leads you into the power of praying specifically for persons and situations. These dynamics, coupled with an emphasis on God's Word and the work of the Holy Spirit, make this plan a useful tool that will make a real difference in your spiritual life.

The Personal Prayer Plan

You are about to enter one of the most exciting journeys in your spiritual life by developing an organized plan to pray. I am convinced that this plan is what most Christians need to use to take their personal ministry of prayer to a new level. This plan will make it simple for you to design your own personal prayer notebook suited to your specific needs.

The first step to put this plan into practice is to make copies of the "Prayer Notebook Outline" provided in the appendix of this book and insert them into a three-ring binder. This simple outline guides you through three steps to follow each day as you meet with God. These steps will become your daily plan for prayer. Just follow them one by one, and you will encounter God in a meaningful way.

It is time for you to begin. God wants to meet with you, so now is the time to implement the plan and go through it step by step. Begin with . . .

Step One: Read God's Word

As I have stated in previous chapters, I believe it is very important to listen to God speak to you daily through His Word. What He says to you in His Word will prepare you to talk to Him and will influence what you say to Him in prayer.

Before you begin to read God's Word, bow your head and be quiet for a few moments. After this brief time of meditation, pray the following prayer: "Lord, speak to me through Your Word now."

Always keep in mind that the Word of God and prayer go hand in hand. As you continue through the prayer outline, keep your Bible open near you.

Now take your time. Let God speak to you through His Word. You may write in your notebook the verses that are meaningful to you so that you can remember them throughout the day.

Always keep in mind that the Word of God and prayer go hand in hand. As you continue through the prayer outline, keep your Bible open near you.

Step Two: Pray

The five talking principles of prayer I described in chapter 1 need to be followed each day after the reading of God's Word. The first principle is . . .

Confession

It is important that you are prepared spiritually before you attempt to have a serious conversation with God. Effective prayer occurs when you talk to God and listen to what God is saying to you. Better communication will result when the lines of communication are clear.

Sin clogs the lines of communication between you and God. Therefore, you need to confess your sin and your helplessness to God. Confession and repentance are very important in the life of the growing Christian. Claim the promise of 1 John 1:9 as you confess your sins. Remember: God hears and answers your prayers when your heart yearns to be clean and right with Him.

The second talking principle of prayer is . . .

Praise

Praise is the expression of your love and adoration for who God is. In this time of praise, focus on three attributes of God's character. You may even take the time to pray through portions of the Scriptures that are filled with praise to God. Make this a rich time of worship between you and your Creator.

The third principle is . . .

Thanksgiving

This is the expression of gratefulness to God for all the things He has done for you. Spend some time offering your thanks to Him for all He has done for you. Thank Him for provisional, physical, and spiritual blessings. Thank Him for people who have blessed you. Take the time to say, "Thanks, God."

The fourth principle is one that comes easily to most of us. It is . . .

Petition

At this time, focus your prayer on personal needs that you want to present to God. Do not pray for others yet; pray for the things you believe to be within God's will for your own life. Record your requests in the space provided in your notebook. As you use your personal prayer notebook, remember to record God's answers to the prayers you lift up to Him both for yourself and for others.

The final principle of prayer is . . .

Intercession

Intercession is the privilege of standing in the gap between the God of heaven and the person you are praying for at the time. Concentrate on praying for the needs of others whom God brings to your mind. Write down each request as you bring it before the Lord. Consider praying for the needs of your family members, your friends, your pastor and his family, and your fellow church members. Remember: God is attracted to the *specific* prayers you pray for yourself and others.

Urgent Requests

During your prayer time, you will also want to list urgent requests that you will pray for every day. An urgent prayer request is so critical that it requires daily attention from you for a specific time or until the crisis has passed. When God places an urgent need in someone else's life upon your heart, commit yourself to pray for that person daily.

> When God places an urgent need in someone else's life upon your heart, commit yourself to pray for that person daily.

Focus-Day Requests

As you become familiar with the basic principles of this plan, you may choose to add an additional layer of intercession that involves focusing your prayer on a special area each day. You may customize your own plan or implement the following schedule:

1. *Sunday: World Missions and Missionaries.* While many of us are not called to full-time missionary work as a career, we are all called by Jesus Christ to make sure the gospel is heard throughout the world. The ministry of prayer can be your involvement in world missions. Pray for the gospel to be taken to the entire world. Many doors need to be opened by the Holy Spirit, and we need to pray for these doors to be opened.

Pray that missionaries, evangelists, and pastors will effectively take the gospel throughout the world.

2. *Monday: Lost and Unchurched.* God wants people to experience life in His Son, Jesus Christ. His desire is not for anyone to perish, but for people across the world to repent of sin and receive Jesus Christ into their lives. On this day, pray for lost and unchurched people by name. Pray for God's direction about whom He wants you to pray for, and write their names and need for salvation in your notebook. Pray for an opportunity to share the gospel of Jesus Christ with these individuals. Pray for an opportunity to invite them to your local church. Also pray for the lost and unchurched people in your area. Ask to see what Jesus sees and to feel what Jesus feels. May the Lord move you to His compassion toward the lost.

3. *Tuesday: United States of America.* Our country is a nation that is in trouble spiritually and morally. Christians need to be committed to praying weekly for their nation. Pray for the gospel to be presented to each person in this country. Pray for spiritual revival and spiritual awakening to happen. Pray for various leaders in America, both nationally and locally (the president, congressmen, the governor of your state, the mayor of your city, your school board officials, and so forth). God will empower you as you pray, and He will give you great insight as you pray for your nation.

4. *Wednesday: Friends.* Jesus was a real friend to His disciples. He loved them and met their needs. Most important, He prayed for them. You can show your love for your friends by praying for them weekly. Pray for God to guide you as you pray for your friends. Ask Him to show you how to pray specifically for

each one. Pray for God to show you how you can minister to these friends by meeting their needs.

5. *Thursday: Christian Leaders.* In recent years, the world has witnessed the moral failure of many Christian leaders. Perhaps much of this has occurred because these people were not covered in prayer by all of God's people. Prayer gives a covering of protection. Prayer gives an empowerment for daily living. Pray for the Lord to put the key Christian leaders on your heart whom He wants you to pray for each week. These may be authors, pastors, evangelists, or influential laypersons. Pray for their continued spiritual success and sphere of influence. Ask God to protect them from moral indiscretion and failure. Pray for their spiritual growth. Your prayers for these leaders will enable them to remain spiritually strong, morally faithful, and totally protected from the missiles of Satan.

6. *Friday: Local Church.* Jesus loves the church. He gave His life for the church. He empowers the church with the Holy Spirit. He entrusts His mission to the church. He prays for the church. Since the church is so important to Jesus, it should be as important to you. Pray for the power of the Holy Spirit to be upon your local church. Pray for your church to be involved in reaching your region, your country, and the world for Jesus. Pray for God's protection to be upon your pastor, your pastor's family, and your local church family. Pray for the worship services and Bible studies that will take place at your church this week. Pray for the Spirit and burden of prayer to come upon your church. Pray for the lay leaders. As you pray, you will begin to see some of these very things take place. Give God the glory and witness to others about the power of prayer.

7. *Saturday: Relatives.* You need to have a legitimate concern for your relatives. You should pray for them, even though you may be separated by great distances or your past experience was negative with some of them. Ask for God's direction as to which relatives to pray for each Saturday. Ask Him to show you their needs so that you can pray for them specifically. If they are unbelievers, pray for their salvation. Pray for God to lead you in how you should minister to them through phone calls, notes, or personal visits. Always close this time of prayer by asking God, "Is there anything You want me to do to nurture any of these relationships?"

When you add focus-day requests to your times of intercession, you will have a healthy balance of prayer. This also will eliminate the hedonistic tendency to concentrate solely upon yourself, even in prayer.

One of the great features of this plan is what happens when it is followed. Not only will you experience quantum leaps in your prayer life, you will also develop a global perspective of the ministry of prayer. As you commit yourself to this personal plan for prayer, I believe that you will develop Jesus' heart for prayer, and your focus in praying for others will become very much like His.

This plan can be customized to fit your specific needs and desires because you write in your own daily prayer requests for yourself and for others. Be careful not to overload this section because too many requests on your prayer list may overwhelm you and even squelch your desire to pray. But remember: Prayer is work!

Step Three: Journal

I believe in the life-changing power of closing your time with God by writing a one-page letter to God. On this one page, you will be recapturing your main burdens as well as the joy of answered prayers. Journaling provides a means of concrete communication with God. It also provides a sense of relief from your burdens. As you document your walk with God in this way, your faith in the power of prayer will increase. Journaling can become one of the greatest dynamics in your prayer life.

Journaling provides a means of concrete communication with God. It also provides a sense of relief from your burdens.

This is a suggested plan intended to help you, not bind you. Feel free to customize it according to your desires. The Holy Spirit will work through this plan, granting you spiritual liberty as you communicate with God. In time, these steps will become natural for you. You can also exchange one step with another. Do not make the plan itself holy. What is holy is when you meet with God in a personal and intimate way every day of your life.

Just Do It!

No longer can you say, "I do not know how to pray." This book has taught you the basic principles about how to pray. Again, regardless of your level of prayer, if you are teachable, you have surely learned something that can add to your prayer life. No longer can you use the excuse that you just do not know what to do in a time with God. This chapter has described in detail how you can develop a personal prayer notebook that is easy to use every day.

So, just do it! Don't make any more excuses in regard to prayer. Now is the time to do what you know you need to do.

If you will follow this plan for prayer, you will experience an immeasurable growth in your spiritual life. If you consistently use this tool over a number of weeks, your lifestyle will never be the same. Enjoy the journey! It's worth it! So, *just do it!*

Appendix ■

PRAYER NOTEBOOK OUTLINE

I. Read _____

II. Pray

    1. Confession

    2. Praise

    3. Thanksgiving

    4. Petition

    5. Intercession

6. Urgent Requests

7. Focus-Day Requests

III. Journal

Date: _____

Dear God,

NOTES

Chapter 1: What Prayer Is All About

1. John F. MacArthur, *The Freedom and Power of Forgiveness* (Wheaton, Ill.: Crossway Books, 1997), 71.

Chapter 7: How to Call upon the Lord

1. Jim Cymbala, *Fresh Wind, Fresh Fire* (Grand Rapids, Mich.: Zondervan Publishing House, 1997), 71–72.
2. J. Paul Reno, *Daniel Nash: Prevailing Prince of Prayer* (Asheville, N.C.: Revival Literature, n.d.), 1–26.

Chapter 8: How to Pray It Through

1. Woodrow Kroll, *When God Doesn't Answer* (Grand Rapids, Mich.: Baker Books, 1997), 157.
2. Ibid.
3. Ibid.

Chapter 11: How to Empower Your Prayers

1. Audio- and videotapes of the June 4, 1995, service and other services at First Baptist Church of Springdale, Arkansas, are

available by calling DayStar Products, (501) 751-4523 or by writing to: DayStar, 1709 Johnson Road, Springdale, Arkansas 72764.

2. For more information about fasting, see the author's previously published book, *The Power of Prayer and Fasting* (Nashville, Tenn.: Broadman and Holman, 1997).

Chapter 12: The Wall of Strained Relationships

1. Oscar Thompson, *Concentric Circles of Concern* (Nashville, Tenn.: Broadman Press, 1981).
2. Warren W. Wiersbe, *Famous Unanswered Prayers* (Lincoln, Nebr.: Back to the Bible, 1986), 11, 13.
3. Kroll, *When God Doesn't Answer,* 65.

Chapter 13: The Wall of Improper Motives

1. Kroll, *When God Doesn't Answer,* 102.

Chapter 14: The Wall of an Unrepentant Heart

1. Kroll, *When God Doesn't Answer,* 32.
2. Adapted from Floyd, *The Power of Prayer and Fasting,* 104–7.